MW00627574

STAND FIRM: WHAT TO DO WHEN LIFE KNOCKS YOU DOWN
ENDORSEMENTS

"I am happy to endorse Dr. Mark Flattery's excellent new book, *Stand Firm: What to Do When Life Knocks You Down*. On every page of this marvelous work, Dr. Flattery shows that the Word of God is our best weapon when we walk 'through the valley of the shadow of death.' Dr. Flattery so convincingly inspires and encourages his readers to take this weapon to their everyday fights in the worst season of life. He also provides direct answer to the question of how to find peace in our life when life feels like a boat floating on the sea where waves of suffering are rolling in endlessly. I very highly recommend this wonderfully inspiring, as well as practical, spiritual book to all Christians."

Younghoon Lee, PhD
Senior Pastor, Yoido Full Gospel Church
Seoul, Korea

"I believe this work portrays the heart-life of the author. It lays out personal and practical guidance in how to STAND regardless of the challenges we face. The meaningful presentation of many biblical texts is enhanced by the vignettes at the beginning of the chapters and the application questions at the end. The author's passion for the broken and hurting is felt by the repeated use of 'you.' This is a great read that calls us to prayer and reminds us of our absolute VICTORY IN CHRIST."

Jack V. Rozell
President, Ministry Resources International

"I've known Mark Flattery for many years, and I am thrilled to recommend his first book, *Stand Firm: What to Do When Life Knocks You Down*. How many know life is going to knock us down at some point? You've felt that. I've felt that. But in the midst of those trials, God's Word shouts, 'The best is yet to come!' It's the struggle that can actually make us stronger, and Mark delivers on these promises from God. That's why I'm so excited for you to read this practical and uplifting book. Through it, Mark shares specific Victory Actions that will draw you closer to God, especially in the seasons of life that bring anxiety, fear, and doubt. I'm hopeful you will find the victory you've been looking for and learn how to fight your battles by God's rules."

Rob Ketterling
Lead Pastor, River Valley Church

"Many people today, Christians included, have suffered knockout blows and can't seem to get back on their feet. Some have quit even trying. Dr. Mark Flattery has a powerful message: Stand Firm. In his new book, Mark draws from the well of his own personal experiences and offers a biblical path to healing, hope, and a renewed sense of purpose. As a personal friend knowledgeable about Mark's own 'knockout' blow, I've been an eyewitness to a man who faithfully followed Jesus through the valley of his pain, suffering and heartache and continues to model a life that shines for the Lord. Mark's passion is to help others Stand Firm. This book will show you 'how.'"

Scott McChrystal
Chaplain (Col) USA (Ret.)

"When life takes you in a very different direction than you could have ever imagined, *Stand Firm: What to Do When Life Knocks You*

Down lets you look over the shoulder of Dr. Mark Flattery for a no-nonsense, biblically based, practical view of what to do and how to respond in the midst of painful difficulties. This book presents a 'road map,' to help the reader to become aware of their end goal, and the step-by-step process to stay biblically grounded amidst the whirling surprises, pain, and incremental victories. I want to thank Dr. Flattery for his transparency to share his story and practical help for the rest of us on the journey."

Donna Barrett
General Secretary, Assemblies of God

"Following a tragedy or natural disaster, everyone longs for hope. We need to know that tomorrow can be better than today, and the pain and suffering will soon pass. In *Stand Firm: What to Do When Life Knocks You Down,* author Mark Flattery provides valuable insights and timely principles based on God's promises. If you are facing hardship now, this book will help you weather the storm and find newfound hope."

Hal Donaldson
President, Convoy of Hope

STAND FIRM

WHAT TO DO WHEN LIFE
KNOCKS YOU DOWN

MARK D. FLATTERY

Cover designed by Jared Deutsch

Published by Network211 in cooperation with Three Clicks Publishing with the permission of Mark Flattery.
3003 E. Chestnut Expressway Ste 2001
Springfield, MO 65802

ISBN 978-1-7330962-8-7

Printed in the United States of America

"Everyone has a plan until they get punched in the mouth,"

Mike Tyson

Professional Boxer

CONTENTS

PREFACE

Do you remember how dreadful you felt when life knocked you down? Heartache. Anxious. Vulnerable. Maybe you are there right now! No one is immune; no one can avoid being knocked to the ground. Whether it be a personal injury that shatters your dreams, a debilitating health issue that shakes you to the core, a financial crisis that crushes your quality of life, or rebuilding after the very personal betrayal of a loved one in divorce, you have been taken to depths that you have never experienced.

My reactions to personal dramas are similar to yours. Sometimes, I either fight my offender or I run away (fight or flight response), while at other times, I am driven to my knees only to feel numb over my entire mind, body, and soul. When we have the feeling that we are being beaten down by life, we can choose to go it alone to find balance or seek help from someone who understands our pain and dilemma and will journey with us.

So where can you find help, hope, and rescue? As you face your life challenge, often feeling isolated and vulnerable, you can find hope and a game plan to victory in the Bible. God's Word will bring you strength, comfort, and inspiration even when you are just trying to survive the moment. I pray that you will also seek solace in the Lord with your church family and with a Christian counselor who can join you in your journey and provide guidance, friendship, and peace.

Stand Firm: What to Do When Life Knocks You Down reveals that God's Word provides a practical and winning game plan when life knocks you down. It offers you reasons to stand, a defensive strategy, and an offensive strategy with victory action steps.

Instead of being victimized and demoralized by the attacks that we all face, God's Word equips you to rise to your feet, stand firm, and live in victory.

I start each chapter with a vignette to set the stage for the content that follows. While watching a boxing match may not be your favorite weekend activity, it is a picture that reminds us that we are in an extremely competitive battle for our lives. Like a boxing match, our encounters are physically taxing, intensely painful, and intimately personal. At some point in our personal journey, what is bad in the world today hits us hard and knocks us to the canvas of life.

The question is: How will we respond?

FOR YOU TO DO

I have some suggestions as to what you should do as you read this book.

1. Ask the Lord to speak to your heart and mind before you begin reading.

2. Read each chapter and then respond to the "For You to Consider" portion.

3. Interact with others about the content. If you work through this book with a small group, you can discuss this material with others, speak encouragement into each other's lives, and hold each other accountable to continue this study and not quit.

4. Write your thoughts in a journal. Many people find "journaling" a helpful response because it forces you to articulate your thoughts in writing and gives you a place to get the burden "off your chest."

5. Memorize God's Word. Each section begins with a Scripture and ends with a Scripture. Please memorize them! Planting God's Word in your heart, mind, and soul will reap a harvest of strength, vibrancy, and resiliency.

THE KNOCKDOWN

"Finally, be strong in the Lord and in the strength of his might. Put on the whole armor of God, that you may be able to stand against the schemes of the devil. For we do not wrestle against flesh and blood, but against the rulers, against the authorities, against the cosmic powers over this present darkness, against the spiritual forces of evil in the heavenly places."

EPHESIANS 6:10–12

It was a typical sultry night at the gym in the tropics. The stench of sweat combined with the high humidity made the evening almost unbearable. A very disinterested audience of ten wasted the night spitting betel nut juice on the seats in front of them. I was surrounded by a gang of young boys who were selling coconuts and old soda bottles left by US soldiers in WW2.

Why was anyone here? There were no cameras, no Internet coverage, no reporters, and well, no one really cared about what happened. And yet, the gladiators inside the roped field of battle warmed up as if their engagement would indeed matter.

The boxer in white shorts called himself "Champ." He had an air of self-confidence that one would expect from a champion, but there were no marks from past fights. He was well groomed and had a physique that was part God-given and part chiseled from hours of tortuous gym workouts. While he made an impressive figure, I doubted seriously that he had ever fought before.

His opponent puzzled me. As he stretched in the left corner of the ring in his red satin shorts, there was nothing physically imposing about him. In fact, he looked rather ordinary. There was no reason to believe that his nickname, which loosely translated meant "Destroyer," was anything but a wishful thought. But as I looked in his eyes, I realized that there was something deeply disturbing about him. He was not just a gym rat who had visions of grandeur. I saw a cold-blooded warrior who was out to maim and brutalize his opponent. This fight was going to quickly get ugly.

As soon as the opening bell rang, I realized that Champ was overconfident. His playful jabs and overblown roundhouse swings were proof that he underestimated his opponent. He assumed his victory simply because he bothered to make an appearance. This was a fatal mistake!

In the third round, Destroyer unleashed a powerful right that astonished Champ completely. The blow landed with such ferocity that it caused the audience to gasp. Champ's knees buckled and he crumbled to the mat. As he lay on the blood-stained canvas, he tried desperately to regain his senses. As if by a miracle, he opened his eyes and sat up. His right hand waved frantically as he struggled to find the ropes. Then, he did something so strange that it will be embedded in my memory forever. He turned and glared at the third man in the ring. Unable to vocalize his thoughts, his piercing eyes glared at the referee as if to convey, "How could you do this to me?"

I assume that you are considering this book because you have experienced a recent crushing defeat that turned your world upside down. You were betrayed, humiliated, isolated, abandoned, embarrassed or a combination of all of these. These feelings are legitimate. But there is a proven, time-tested response that will get you off the canvas and on the winning path. There are some points from my story that I want to emphasize as we start our journey together.

First, whether you want to recognize it or not, you are in a spiritual battle for your eternal destiny. I know that this sounds overstated, but the truth is the devil is out to get you and will do everything he can to rob you of the life that God created you to live.

The devil knows that he is a created being who was thrown from heaven due to his disobedience and pride. He knows that he cannot overpower God or directly impact God in any way. Instead, he focuses his attacks on those who are most precious to God—His children: you and me. His strategy is to seek and destroy, in a spiritual battle, those created in God's image as the means to hurt God.

> **You are in a spiritual battle for your eternal destiny. . . . The devil is out to get you and will do everything he can to rob you of the life that God created you to live.**

The spiritual battle is manifested flagrantly in the religious persecution going on in our world today. We hear stories of believers who are tortured and whose families are killed simply because they declared their love for Jesus or they were caught with a Bible. Our hearts cry out for them. We know from God's Word that He will not let them die in vain. He will balance the scales of justice as He rewards the righteous and punishes the wicked.

The battle that you face right now, however, is probably not due to religious persecution and for that we should all be humbled and thankful. I do not want to diminish in any way the sacrifices that these believers make for the sake of the Gospel. At the same time, I suggest to you that your current battle is equally important to God because the eternal consequences are the same.

The spiritual battle you are facing may be due to a recent trauma or tragedy. You are in a battle. You may be struggling to find a new job so that you can support your family. You are in a battle. You may still be in shock when your life turned into a nightmare because your spouse abandoned the marriage vows and had an affair. You are in a battle. You may have been devastated deeply by the death of a loved one. You are in a battle.

You are in a battle when you are tempted to be less than who God created you to be.

Your spiritual battle may be waged in the routines of life. You may feel like you are drowning in a sea of red ink when you sit at your desk to pay your monthly bills. You are in a battle. You are in a battle whenever you surf the Internet or flip through TV channels. You are in a battle when you are in a conversation that turns into gossip or to speak of someone in ways that is demeaning or belittling. You are in a battle when you are tempted to be less than who God created you to be.

You are in a spiritual battle whether you recognize it or not. I hope that you will be alert to this fact and prepare for life's encounters. Let me remind you right now that you will get hit. Life will knock you down. It happens to all of us at some point in our lives.

Second, once you realize that you are in a battle you must identify who hurt you. One of the first questions you will ask when life knocks you down is, "Why?" Oddly, the frequent first response for us is to get mad at God! It is amazing to me that when life falls apart, we automatically blame God, wonder what He is doing, question His motives, and ask aloud if He really cares. This anger is misplaced for God is not the author of confusion or anxiety. He does not condemn or act rashly. While the one who hurt you may be your boss, your friend, your spouse, someone you do not know, or it may even be a natural disaster, the source of all things bad is the devil. So instead of turning away from God, get mad at the devil for ultimately, he is the one who punched you in the mouth.

Third, this constant battle deserves your serious attention and a strategic response. You can play around with your spiritual health and give it a half-hearted effort, or you can engage the Trinity wholeheartedly and stand firm in even the most ferocious battles. The only genuinely viable course of action is to turn completely to Jesus Christ. Everything else—learned cultural **Are you willing to regroup and rebuild? Are you willing to put aside your pain and pride and build a winning strategy around Jesus Christ?** responses, TV and talk radio psychology experts, tabloid magazines, self-help books, and dabbling into other recognized or false religions—will fall woefully short in equipping you with a winning strategy to impact your future.

If you were to share your story with me right now, you would likely focus on the injustice done to you, the tragedy of the situation, and the resulting wounds. It is human nature for the focal point of your account to be the sins of your offender. As horrible as your offender may be, the only way that you will get off the canvas of life is to focus on you. Are you willing to regroup and rebuild?

Are you willing to put aside your pain and pride and build a winning strategy around Jesus Christ?

At this point you might be thinking, "Hang on a minute! I am the one who was hurt and abused. What do you mean that I must put aside my pride and pain?" Well, the truth is you cannot make your offender change. There is nothing whatsoever you can do or say to make your offender repent or change his or her behavior. The only one you can change is you. You cannot change what already happened to you. But you can change your actions and reactions today and therefore build a strong tomorrow. In the following chapters, let's examine the Scriptures together and talk about how you can stand firm when life knocks you down.

FOR YOU TO CONSIDER

1. What happened that knocked you to the canvas of life?

2. Describe your feelings at that time and how you responded.

3. In retrospect, did you respond rightly and what would you do differently, if you could?

4. Are you willing to hear from God's Word to help you right now?

SCRIPTURE FOR YOU TO PRAY TODAY

"For God hath not given us the spirit of fear; but of power, and of love, and of a sound mind" (2 Timothy 1:7, KJV).

What is the Lord saying to you right now?

1

TEN REASONS TO GET UP AND STAND FIRM

"When Jesus saw him lying there and knew that he had already been there a long time, he said to him, 'Do you want to be healed?'"

JOHN 5:6

As Champ sat on the canvas trying to regain control of his mind and his body, I questioned seriously if he would get up. *The true test of a boxer is not the ferocious force he can create with his signature right hook, but rather, can he take a punch? Does the Champ really want to get up and face another pounding? I wondered what it would take for him to rise and face again his seemingly undefeatable foe.*

If I just had my face crushed, I would question my motivation for being in the ring and even consider the merits of throwing in the towel. What would motivate Champ to get up? The money cannot be enough to compensate the physical torture. Does he love the sport so much that he is willing to continue to get beaten? Maybe he is a complete idiot who loves pain and has no idea of the impact it will have on his body later in life. Whatever his motivation, if Champ wanted to win this match and continue his boxing career, then he had to get up.

Certainly, the crowd's response did not encourage the battered boxer to reenter the fight. Two men whistled loudly expressing their disgust. Screaming, the man closest to me threw banana peelings into the ring. The boys in the crowd ran ringside, heckling Champ.

If I were a betting man, I would say that there was no chance whatsoever of Champ getting up. As his blood and sweat poured from his face, it seemed that he had no more fight left in him. The next few seconds would reveal his character and determine his future.

I have always thought that the true test of a man's character is not how he revels in victory but how he responds in the face of crushing defeat. Anyone can have a strong sense of self-worth when surrounded by adoring friends in the mountaintop experiences of life. But when you get pounded into the canvas of life and are trying to regain your senses, you are at a crossroads. How desperately do you want to get up? What is your true reason for living? What are your hopes and dreams now? Are you willing to get up and fight for them?

Chapter 5 of the Gospel of John records an encounter at the pool of Bethesda between Jesus and a man who had been an invalid for thirty-eight years. The man was one of a great number who had been knocked down by life: the "blind, the lame, the paralyzed" (John 5:3).

Jesus, knowing that this man had battled physical challenges for a long time, asked him an interesting question: "Do you want to get well?"

Let's stop and consider this question. "Do you want to get well?" It seems obvious that the man was in a hopeless state and that he would give everything he had to be healed. And yet, there are people who have been lying on the canvas of life so far beyond the ten count that the knock-down punch became the knockout punch. They identify now so closely with the tragedy in their lives that they have a new and, well, we can use the word warped, sense of normalcy. The knockout punch defines them now. Their life started with life's blow, and everything else is viewed in retrospect from the mental movies of that fateful moment.

Right now, you are hurting. You are hurting from the life blow that either came from someone you trusted or it involved someone that you love. Your pain is legitimate and should not be trivialized or marginalized in any way. You are on

Do you really want the tragedy to define you and to rob you of the life that God created you to live?

the canvas of life because someone, or something, hurt you deeply. I understand your pain. But the question then becomes, "Do you want to get well?"

If you stay down then you allow your offender to bring pain to your life daily and even beyond as the moment will have a ripple effect on all those in your sphere of influence. For example, we hear stories of parents who lost a child to a disease, then expressed such rage and bitterness toward God that it poisoned their children who lived and debilitated their children's personal relationship with Him.

Do you really want the tragedy to define you and to rob you of the life that God created you to live? If you want to be healed, then you must do what Jesus told the man in John 5 to do: "Get up, take up your bed, and walk" (John 5:8). The man turned to Jesus, received instruction, and was obedient to do what Jesus told him to do. And look at what happened: "At once the man was healed, and he took up his bed and walked" (John 5:9).

This man's story can be your testimony. But you must be willing to stand! Let's consider ten reasons why you can, and should, stand. We will consider how standing impacts you personally and then how your desire to get well influences others who are in your life.

TEN REASONS TO GET UP AND STAND FIRM AFTER LIFE KNOCKED YOU DOWN

1. You must stand because your life depends on it.

We discussed this already but it needs to be addressed again. Whatever happened to you was horrible. It may have been undeserved completely and it was wrong. But even if the offense was your fault, you cannot allow yourself to wallow in self-pity or to stay down. If you stay down, then it is over; you are defeated. The one who knocked you down wins because you were knocked out. This will define you for the rest of your life.

You must get up and live another day. If you are willing to be healed, then God will provide the means to overcome the defeat, to learn from the defeat, and use the defeat as fuel to live a meaningful and fulfilling life. God's work in your life is so powerful that there is a guarantee: If you submit your heart and will to Jesus in this dark hour, you will grow closer in your relationship with Him. You will be amazed how He will turn what was meant for evil into good. The road to a thriving life begins with "Get up, take up your bed, and walk." You must stand because your life depends on it!

2. You must stand because you are equipped by God to stand.

I remember the first time I jumped off the high dive at the local swimming pool. I was about nine or ten years old at the time. I was deathly afraid of heights and was not at all a strong swimmer. However, I let the taunts of my brother's friend get me at the high dive and manipulated me into the most death-defying act of my life up to that point. I was scared as I climbed the ladder. I was speechless as I surveyed the view from such epic heights. I remember praying and asking the Lord that if he would forgive me for my stupidity and allow me to survive that I would never, ever do something that crazy again. I did find the courage to jump. It seemed like a fraction of a second until I hit the water and plunged into the deep end. I was surprised that I almost touched the bottom of the pool. I was prepared for this adventure at this juncture. However, I was utterly unprepared for the eternity it took for my body to make it back to the surface. I could not breathe! I knew enough to keep my mouth closed for if I opened it I would swallow water and drown. My body would remain then in the bottom of the pool and it would not be found until they drained it at the end of the summer. So I kicked my arms and legs and fought for my life! I struggled and finally cut through the surface gasping for air.

Your knock-down punch left you feeling isolated and alone. You feel as if you are the only one who has had to endure such punishment at this moment. You had plans, dreams, visions, and ambitions which were all built on the premise that you will succeed! But that came to a crashing halt and you are wondering if you will ever be the same again. Like my diving story, you feel that you were forcibly submerged and seeking desperately for the day when you can reach the surface and just breathe again.

You probably do not realize it, but God has equipped you to breathe again and stand in spite of your circumstances. The first part of 1 Corinthians 10:13 teaches us that, "No temptation has overtaken you that is not common to man. God is faithful, and he will not let you be tempted beyond your ability." Your spiritual battle is not fought outside of God's view. He sees what has happened to you. He knows your mental and physical battle. He knows what your future will be! While you feel as if you are the only one enduring your difficulties, the truth is that you are not the first one to encounter this battle and you will not be the last one either. God really is protecting you and will not allow you to drown in a sea of despair. His protection keeps you from being overrun by sin, and His Word will be your strength to overcome this current trial. If you will be faithful to God, then He will be faithful to you, and thus, you will find His strength to get up and stand again.

You probably do not realize it, but God has equipped you to breathe again and stand in spite of your circumstances.

God's promise to Joshua applies to you in this very moment. "Just as I was with Moses, so I will be with you. I will not leave you or forsake you." (Joshua 1:5b). God will never leave you nor forsake you! You are equipped to stand again if you will align yourself with God because His presence in your life is a guarantee; you can bet your life on it! You are equipped to stand!

3. You must stand because Jesus is fighting for you.

The completion of 1 Corinthians 10:13 provides hope; "but with the temptation he will also provide the way of escape, that you may be able to endure it." God provided you a way out of your nightmare! There is hope that your circumstances will change.

There is hope that this season of suffering will end and that you will dream and soar once again. But the foundation of your future is not built on your abilities to stand again and to fight. In fact, the secret of your success will be not to summon your inner strength but to release the entirety of your being to Jesus Christ and to live by His rules. The exit sign from your predicament leads you to Jesus.

Matthew 11:28–30 records a teaching by Jesus that speaks clearly to you right now. "Come to me, all who labor and are heavy laden, and I will give you rest. Take my yoke upon you, and learn from me, for I am gentle and lowly in heart, and you will find rest for your souls. For my yoke is easy, and my burden is light."

You are weary and burdened by the battle. You can find rest in Jesus. He is the Master Teacher who loves you so much that He died for your sins. If you submit your heart and your will to Him and if you are obeying Him, then you will find the way out of your trial and you will find rest. If you are willing to live your life by following Jesus completely, then you will be able to stand again because He will be your strength and He will fight your battles for you. Jesus provided you the way to stand!

4. You must stand because God will make something good from your personal drama.

More than likely you cannot see how anything good can come from your present adversity. Humanly speaking, that thought is absolutely correct. However, you are not limited to responding humanly for you have God as your friend. I encourage you to take your eyes off your problem and the subsequent depressing view of life. Instead, focus on the Answer and the resulting hope that waits for you. God will make something good from your pain if only you will let Him.

The apostle Paul's letter to the Romans is your promise today; "And we know that for those who love God all things work together for good, for those who are called according to his purpose." (Romans 8:28). God is on your side and will turn all things for your good. It is an easy task for God to turn all the joys and abundance of life into your good because those items are already packaged as blessings. While we are thankful for all the blessings given to us, and we count them as gifts from God, you must realize that He will take the worst situations of life and turn them to your good. He can take your horrible, rotten, disgusting situation and find good.

Does this mean that you will get your job back? Will your spouse repent and come home? Will you be freed from disease and be healed? Well, these events can happen and certainly we would consider that as good. But if our desired outcomes are not met that does not mean that God is absent, uncaring, or uninvolved. Sometimes, we must have faith to walk with the Lord, to allow Him to break us of our stubbornness and self-reliance, and to allow Him to re-create us in His image. What this means is if you turn to the Lord then the good that you receive starts with His powerful presence in your heart and continues as he molds you into the person of God that He desires you to be.

You may not be able to see what good will come from this trial. Yet you can stand in faith and know that God will fight for you and bring good. Your reason for doing so lies solely in the fact you are standing on the promise found in God's Word. You may not see the good, you may not feel it in your heart, and you many not experience it yet, but the good will come if you continue to love the Lord and fulfill His calling on our life. You must stand because God is not finished with you yet, and He will make something good!

5. You must stand because when you do you will be stronger for it.

When life knocked you down you had your pride hurt. You were humiliated. You were defeated. Maybe you thought, *This isn't supposed to happen to me!* or *Everything I touch is supposed to turn to gold!* or *I don't deserve this!* It is true that you were punched and you were knocked down. That is the fact. If you do get back on your feet and stand with Jesus, then you will discover you will be stronger for the experience. As much as we disdain adversity, we cannot discover who we truly are without a test or a trial.

You will be stronger spiritually if you align your priorities and values with Jesus during this season, then the Lord will take what was meant for evil and turn it to good. If you do so you will discover what matters most. The most important parts of life are not money, status, or glory.

> **You will be stronger spiritually if you align your priorities and values with Jesus during this season, then the Lord will take what was meant for evil and turn it to good.**

Rather, the most important parts of life are loving God and loving others. Your love for God is expressed by your unrelenting trust and wholehearted commitment to Him during the most difficult of times. Your love for others is expressed as you continue to love in spite of your surroundings and in a manner that leads others closer in their walk with the Lord.

Each time you stand after being injured becomes a foundational experience that God will use to build you to be a better person. You will become better from the experience if you learn the lessons that you were supposed to learn and make the necessary changes. Each experience can be a monument in your heart as to how life was bad, but God is good, and He led you through to a season of victory.

One day, hopefully soon, your present season of grief will end, and you will be stronger because you turned yourself over to Jesus and allowed Him to weather the storm. Then you will be prepared the next time life tries to knock you down because you can remember the victory of the past. Your personal history will fuel you with encouragement to act rightly in your next battle because God, who was faithful in the past, is faithful today, and He will be faithful tomorrow. You must stand because you will be stronger as a result!

6. You must stand because the pain from the defeat will lessen eventually and a new season will come if you stand.

You may feel like you are stuck in a rut and that all the energy you are expending amounts to nothing more that spinning your wheels and digging you deeper into your entrapment. Or maybe you feel like Sisyphus from Greek mythology whose punishment was to roll a huge rock up a steep hill only to have it roll back before reaching the summit. He was forced to repeat this again and again, dooming him to an eternity of never ending frustration. Will this misery ever end?

What is most debilitating in your current situation is that you have lost hope that your life will ever be pain free. You may have exhausted your abilities to change your context and now see no way out. You are stuck in a nightmare with no hope. But as one who experienced life knock downs, I will ask you to do something that a friend asked me to do when I was at the lowest of my lowest point: remember that this season will pass.

You may not believe me now, but if you turn your mind and heart to Jesus and follow Him completely then you will discover that He will turn the page in your present drama and take you to a new life chapter. In John 10:10, we read that Jesus said, "I came that they may have life and have it abundantly." If you follow the Lord now, then He will get you out of the rut and back on the road again.

I encourage you to be patient and remember that the Lord is moving on your behalf even though you may not see tangible evidence. We call that "faith." Hebrews 11:1 provides the biblical definition of faith: "Now faith is the assurance of things hoped for, the conviction of things not seen." If you will ask God for the strength to stand and live fully again then you must be certain that this season of turmoil will pass and that you will live to see a new day.

One of my favorite episodes in the Book of Acts is the account of Paul and Silas in chapter 16. They walked fully in the Lord's will as they ministered in Philippi. Paul commanded a demon to leave a slave girl that resulted in him and Silas being seized, humiliated in the marketplace, threatened, stripped, beaten, severely flogged, and thrown into prison. If anyone had the right to be depressed and give up on life, it was Paul and Silas at that moment! Even though they had no hope, humanly speaking, we read, "About midnight Paul and Silas were praying and singing hymns to God" (Acts 16:25). They were not held captive by human limitations for they knew that this incident was not the final chapter of their lives. They had faith that God was greater than their trials and that someway and somehow, He would bring change.

"Suddenly" (Acts 16:26), an earthquake hit, the chains broke open, and Paul and Silas were freed! These events led to the salvation of the jailer and his household. Paul and Silas knew that God was working behind the scenes to fulfill His plan and that He would turn what was meant for evil into good and that good was the salvation of many lives. In a similar way, this can be your story, too! I encourage you to stand because the pain of your defeat will expire and you will experience a new season!

Here are some reasons why you must get up and stand as it relates to people in your life whom you influence:

7. You must stand because the Family of God needs you to stand.

There is a great spiritual battle being fought through the ages for the hearts and destinies of humanity. The enemy wants you to believe that what you do impacts you alone and that no one cares. This is an outright lie. Jesus Christ knows your thoughts before you think them and knew you even before you were born. He died for your sins so that you can be in right relationship with the Father. He died and rose again for you. You matter!

You matter to God and your life matters to the family of God! Imagine that you are standing in front of one of Europe's grand cathedrals. You would be impressed by the size of the stones and the number of stones used in building the church. A few stones on top of each other does not do much. When the stones are placed strategically by a master architect, then you see that he has built a beautiful place of worship! God, the Master Architect, is doing the same with His Church.

Jesus told Peter that he was a rock and on that rock He would build His Church (Matthew 16:18), Later, Peter wrote that we are each living stones who are being built into a spiritual house (1 Peter 2:4–5) and that Jesus is the Cornerstone (1 Peter 4:6). Christ lives in each rock individually and in the rocks collectively because He placed them together to form His Church— the family of God. But just as in real life when a rock is missing from the cathedral and leaves a gap that exposes the entire building to the outside elements, the Church is weakened by your absence because it was designed to have you fully functioning in the right location. It is strongest when all rocks are present and in their proper place. As each stone matters to the architect building a beautiful cathedral that will stand for centuries, you matter to Jesus as He builds His Church to impact this world until the end of time.

You may think, What does it matter if I don't stand? The Church will move on without me. While there is truth to that, it is a negative statement that devalues you. Remember that you are so valuable that Christ died for you, and therefore, you matter!

A better question to ask is, "What will happen if each of us stands?" The reality is that the spiritual battle is waged in one heart at a time. If you get up and stand firm and if I do the same and stand with you in agreement, then together we are a living example of Ecclesiastes 4:12, "And though a man might prevail against one who is alone, two will withstand him—a threefold cord is not quickly broken." We need you to stand!

As we are in the family of God together, your victory encourages me. Our shared experiences teach us to live rightly by God's standards. Our journey through life together brings strength, encouragement, and resiliency. The great spiritual battle is won one person at a time. Not only do you matter to God, but you matter of the entire family of God!

8. You must stand because the people you influence depend on it.

Those in your circle of influence need you stand. Your children, family, and friends are impacted deeply by what happened to you. In fact, people you barely know, like your coworkers and other believers who hear your story are touched by what happened to you. Your ability to stand in righteousness is an outward testimony of your inner relationship with Jesus Christ. If you choose to quit or if you choose to respond in an unrighteous manner, then it reflects badly on Jesus Christ and negatively influences those in your inner circle. But your choice to stand and to follow God's rules will be a testimony that He can get you through any trial or difficulty.

Too often we hear stories of a married person having an affair just to get back at a spouse who had an adulterous relationship. The children are caught in the middle of this insanity and often are forced to take sides. But who will stand for the children and say, "Follow me as I follow Christ"?[1] Children need their parents to walk righteously, to love unconditionally, to discipline in love, and to set a proper example of how to live. They need the offended parent to show them how to behave in good times, but most importantly, in the bad times of life as well. Such an example will provide security for them as children and equip them to deal properly with adversity as adults. The ones in your circle of influence need you to stand!

9. You must stand because you can then help others when they are knocked down.

It is interesting that when life knocks you down you are tempted to believe that you are the only one enduring this humiliation. This is an untruth, a lie. There have been hundreds of books written about your situation because there were thousands, if not millions, of people who have endured your exact defeat. You are not the first to get knocked down and you certainly will not be the last one! But if you find your will to stand and stand righteously, you will be equipped to speak with authority into the lives of others who get knocked down by life. Your story can be that although you were lost in the chaos of despair, you let Jesus re-create your life, and now you can lead others to the Answer that they need so desperately.

In his letter to the church at Corinth, Paul wrote, "We are afflicted in every way, but not crushed; perplexed, but not driven to despair; persecuted, but not forsaken; struck down, but not

---

1 See 1 Corinthians 11:1.

destroyed; always carrying in the body the death of Jesus, so that the life of Jesus may also be manifested in our bodies. For we who live are always being given over to death for Jesus' sake, so that the life of Jesus also may be manifested in our mortal flesh" (2 Corinthians 4:8–11). Right now, you may feel crushed, perplexed, persecuted, stuck down, and even forsaken. But Paul is teaching you that even though you feel this way, since Jesus stands with you, then you are not crushed, in despair, abandoned, or destroyed. You may be thinking, *That's fine, but has Paul endured my suffering?*

I believe that Paul understood your situation and is imminently qualified to address it because he was a man accustomed to pain and suffering. Turn to 2 Corinthians 11:23–29 and you will see a list of Paul's sufferings; flogged severely, exposed to death frequently, five times he was beaten within an inch of his life, three times beaten by rods, stoned, three times shipwrecked, sleep deprived, exposed to the elements, experiencing hunger and thirst, and the list goes on. "Who is weak, and I am not weak? Who is made to fall, and I am not indignant?" (2 Corinthians 11:29). In other words, Paul can relate to your defeat! Like you, Paul was knocked down by life. But look at how he responded! He wrote that in our moments of weakness, Christ Jesus will be our strength and that His power is made perfect in our weakness (2 Corinthians 12:9). Paul then stated, "For the sake of Christ, then, I am content

> **Right now, you may feel crushed, perplexed, persecuted, stuck down, and even forsaken. But Paul is teaching you that even though you feel this way, since Jesus stands with you, then you are not crushed, in despair, abandoned, or destroyed.**

with weaknesses, insults, hardships, persecutions, and calamities. For when I am weak, then I am strong" (2 Corinthians 12:10).

So Paul knows about that which he speaks when he wrote that when he was knocked down, he was not knocked out because Christ is his strength. This can be your story, too! The life of Jesus will be revealed in your testimony if you are willing to stand and help those who follow in your footsteps.

When you stand to declare, "I love the Lord more than life itself," you are stating that in spite of what happened to you and in spite of your current limited view of your situation, you trust in the Lord that He will take care of you.

What happened to you is tragic. But a greater tragedy will be if you do not stand and allow your experience to benefit others. While our situations may be different, we serve the same God who will help us to stand. So stand and let your words be to those who follow you and those you influence: "It is what it is, but God who helped me, will help you!"

10. You must stand because it glorifies Jesus Christ.

I pray that by now you made the decision to get off the canvas and stand firm to fight another day. Hopefully, you do not need another reason, but if you do then we must consider the best reason: to glorify Jesus Christ. When you stand with Jesus you allow your faith in God to define you instead of being characterized by your accomplishments, possessions, reputation, or even your defeats. This glorifies the Lord. When you stand to declare, "I love the Lord more than life itself," you are stating that in spite of what happened to you and in spite of your current limited view of your situation, you trust in the Lord that He will take care of you. This glorifies the Lord.

The Old Testament prophet Habakkuk wrote it this way, "Though the fig tree should not blossom, nor fruit be on the vines, the produce of the olive fail and the fields yield no food, the flock be cut off from the fold and there be no herd in the stalls, yet I will rejoice in the LORD; I will take joy in the God of my salvation" (Habakkuk 3:17–18). Though everything is taken from you and you are left seemingly with nothing, yet you can rejoice in the Lord. This attitude glorifies Jesus.

I imagine that you are asking, "This sounds good, but how do I do it?" I understand that you have been knocked off balance. No one expects you to be doing the Dance of Joy after getting punched in the mouth by life. So I recommend that you memorize Habakkuk 3:17–18, and make it a daily declaration, offering as much rejoicing and joy in the Lord that you can muster. Today, this may be only a statement, but as you build on it, you will soon develop that statement into an attitude and then that attitude into a lifestyle.

The Lord's disciples were trapped in a similar dilemma when His teaching was so perplexing and even counter-intuitive to their understanding that the crowds were turning away. The disciples were just as confused by the teaching as the crowds were, and yet they loved Jesus. Jesus asked them, "Do you want to go away as well?" (John 6:67). This was a defining moment in the disciples' lives. Peter answered in a manner similar to Habakkuk when he declared, "Lord, to whom shall we go? You have the words of eternal life, and we have believed, and have come to know, that you are the Holy One of God" (John 6:68–69).

You may still be struggling with the reality that you have been knocked down. This is the exact time to get off the canvas and stand! I encourage you to take your focus off your weaknesses and turn your eyes to Jesus, the One who is the very definition of love and truth. Jesus has the words of eternal life. He is your Answer right now. When you stand with Him, you will glorify Him!

"Do you want to get well?" I believe that you do! Use my ten reasons to stand as a springboard of ideas and list your own reasons. You do not have to be a victim anymore. Get up, stand firm, and make the proper response! What you need now is a game plan, a road map, that will take you from where you are now to where you need to be.

The action plan you need to stand firm again is found in God's Word. We will start by considering your battle from a defensive perspective ("what happened?") so that you will not get pummeled again. Then, we will engage an offensive tactic that may surprise you. It may not be the strategy that you would engage naturally, but it is a tactic proven to be powerfully effective and is battle tested throughout history.

FOR YOU TO CONSIDER

1. Do you want to get well or do you want to continue to stay on the canvas of life? What are you willing release from your life and what must you add to your life that will lead you toward wellness?

2. Choose three of the reasons "why you must stand" that resonated with you. Explain why they made an impression on you and what will be your response to each one.

3. Make a list of people that you know and consider how they will be impacted if you do not stand. Consider how those same people will be influenced positively if you do get off the canvas of life and stand to your feet.

4. List at least three reasons to rejoice or be thankful. Even in your current predicament, counting your blessings can positively change your attitude.

SCRIPTURE FOR YOU TO PRAY TODAY

"And we know that for those who love God all things work together for good, for those who are called according to his purpose" (Romans 8:28).

What is the Lord saying to you right now?

2

THE DEFENSIVE STRATEGY

"No temptation has overtaken you that is not common to man. God is faithful, and he will not let you be tempted beyond your ability, but with the temptation he will also provide the way of escape, that you may be able to endure it."

1 CORINTHIANS 10:13

I was amazed that Champ found the inner strength to get off the canvas and stagger to his corner. His manager frantically checked his vital signs to ensure that his protégé was still dealing with reality. He tried to get Champ's attention to discuss strategy, but could not because Champ was ranting at his opponent. Why was he wasting precious time blaming the ref and taunting his opponent? He should have been trying to figure out how he opened himself to a potential knockout blow and planning a defensive strategy to avoid getting his face pounded into the canvas again.

Apparently, the manager and I were on the same page. Though I no idea what he was saying, I did not need a translator to understand his message. He gritted his teeth, got nose to nose and eyeball to eyeball to the boxer, and shouted so loudly that his face turned bright crimson. He was so forceful that everyone in the stands heard him loud and clear. It caused the man seated in front of me to double over and choke on his betel nut juice. He finally got Champ's attention. The boxer stared back and nodded his head three times in agreement.

The bell rang to start round four. Champ leaped to his feet with renewed energy and anticipation. He had taken Destroyer's best blow and survived.

It only took a few punches for his opponent to realize that Champ was a different boxer. It was as if someone flipped a switch as he morphed from being a puncher to a fighter. Lady momentum just switched sides.

Y ou were knocked to the canvas of life by a punch that caught you by surprise. You probably should have seen it coming, and in fact, deep down you knew the possibility of a knock-out blow was there. Yet it was a surprise nonetheless. Now, you must regain your senses and stand. You do not have to stay down. This tragedy does not have to define you! The battle can be won!

If you are like me, then you might be inclined to ask, "What just happened?" As you rehash the episode of the "train wreck" to your friends, you will probably relive in great detail the events that caused you pain, and specifically the vile behavior and malevolent motives of your offender. However, if you continue to focus your heart and mind on your offender and the tragic offense, then the event will soon begin to define you. You cannot live fully in the present or hope in the future if you are chained to the past.

The first step to win the battle is to regain your balance by recovering from the past. It is like the boxer in our story who stopped blaming the referee and his opponent, and began focusing inwardly to learn from his mistakes and implement a new strategy. Let's consider this in another way. Before you can get on the offensive and enforce your will, you must first discover impenetrable defensive tactics or you will suffer a subsequent blow. That hit could prove to be the knockout punch; one from which you would never recover.

You must reposition yourself in your walk with the Lord and shine the spotlight inwardly so that you can learn from your personal drama and emerge in victory as a better person.

Thankfully, your quest for a classic defense was detailed already in the New Testament Book of James. In chapter four, James discussed the reasons for fighting and quarreling in the Church. Believers proclaimed that they were disciples of Christ, but their actions revealed that they were instead friends with "the world." James called the saints to back away from their personal battles and vendettas and focus instead on God. I believe that James' admonition to his readers presents a invaluable defensive strategy for you to implement personally.

James 4:7–11 is a strong call for you to focus on you first. Then, and only then, will you be prepared to launch a counter-attack. You must reposition yourself in your walk with the Lord and shine the spotlight inwardly so that you can learn from your personal drama and emerge in victory as a better person.

Submit yourselves therefore to God. Resist the devil, and he will flee from you. Draw near to God, and he will draw near to you. Cleanse your hands, you sinners, and purify your hearts, you double-minded. Be wretched and mourn and weep. Let your laughter be turned to mourning and your joy to gloom. Humble yourselves before the Lord, and he will exalt you. Do not speak evil against one another, brothers. The one who speaks against a brother or judges his brother, speaks evil against the law and judges the law." (James 4:7–11a).

The eleven directives in this passage are the linchpins in your recovery and will springboard you to a strategic pathway to a victorious life.

1. SUBMIT YOURSELVES THEREFORE TO GOD.

Submit does not mean just to allow God to speak into your life. It does not mean only that you will start now to obey fully his commands. Submit means to empty yourself completely of everything that comprises "you." Like a person dying of thirst and craving water, you must seek then to be filled with the presence of God in your heart and mind.

It has been said that the definition of insanity is doing the same thing over and over again, expecting different results. Another saying is that you cannot use the same mind-set to solve a problem as the mind-set that created the problem. You tried to find your sense of balance on your terms and in your way. Like the Israelites wandering in the desert for forty years, your efforts were futile and brought no lasting results.

Doubling your efforts, pulling yourself up by your bootstraps, and using mind games like refusing to deal with reality and thinking only positive thoughts have all fallen short of the joy and peace that you desire so deeply. You can even set new boundaries with rules and regulations. While these may have a short-term improvement, it lacks lasting effect. Colossians 2:23 says, "These have indeed an appearance of wisdom in promoting self-made religion and asceticism and severity to the body, but they are of no value in stopping the indulgence of the flesh." These efforts will not produce the lasting change that you need because you are still trying to be in control and manipulate life to obtain *your* desired outcome.

It is now time to try a different approach. It is time to give your problem, your burden, and your pain over to the One who is infinitely able to deal with your situation and place you on His road to fulfilling the destiny He has for you. It is time to submit to God.

It is time to give your problem, your burden, and your pain over to the One who is infinitely able to deal with your situation and place you on His road to fulfilling the destiny He has for you. It is time to submit to God.

Submission means that you will empty your will, your pride, and your desires, and seek to be filled to overflowing with the presence of God. Ask that His kingdom come and His will be done in your life.[1] Live by His rules. Live by His standards. Seek His Will for your life and for the lives of all those you influence. With the apostle Paul, declare, "I have been crucified with Christ. It is no longer I who live, but Christ who lives in me. And the life I now live in the flesh I live by faith in the Son of God, who loved me and gave himself for me" (Galatians 2:20). This is what it means to submit.

1 Matthew 6:10.

If you are not willing to submit completely to God, you will be doomed to an endless cycle of reliving the past and playing the role of the wounded victim. You will be a modern version of Sisyphus, the character in Greek mythology I mentioned in chapter one. Remember, his punishment was to roll a huge boulder up a hill only to see it roll back again. He was doomed to repeat this for the rest of eternity. Your nightmare can be broken only by submitting your heart, mind, and will to Jesus and asking Him to take control of your life.

Read Psalm 139:23–24 now and offer it as a prayer to the Lord:

> *Search me, God, and know my heart; test me and know my anxious thoughts. See if there is any offensive way in me, and lead me in the way everlasting (NIV).*

2. RESIST THE DEVIL, AND HE WILL FLEE FROM YOU.

Once you take a stand for God there is nothing that the devil can do except flee. The devil cannot be around people who are submitted fully to God. There is nothing more the devil cannot stand than a person who loves God more than life itself. When you refuse to fight by the devil's rules, when you seek to be committed totally to God, and when you refuse to get revenge and hurt those who hurt you, then the only action left for the devil to do is to flee and seek to fight another day. Like Joshua, you can declare, "As for me and my house, we will serve the LORD" (Joshua 24:15).

Resisting the devil goes far beyond rebuking him or say, "I resist you," even though you have good intentions. Resisting the devil requires the self-discipline to say "No!" to the devil's temptation and doubts and to respond instead with thoughts and actions that are righteous. Let's consider the idea of revenge as an example.

You may have been tempted to respond initially to the one who hurt you by attempting to hurt him or her even more. The temptation may be so strong that you are forced to fight an internal battle about whether or not to react in a way that the world would deem appropriate. You may then be trapped in a mindset that such a reaction is not only justified but actually needed because you want to teach your offender a lesson. Suddenly, you go from being offended to being judge, jury, and executioner, and then, of all things, your revenge quest causes you to be the offender. This downward spiral from offended to offender leads to vendettas and cause everyone to lose. It becomes a classic "lose-lose" situation!

But the Book of James tells us that, in order to end this cycle that can lead only to tragedy, you must resist the devil. You resist by acting righteously. We will go into greater detail about acting righteously later in this book, but for now, I will mention that acting righteously means that you will do the right action, for the right reason, for the right outcome, and for the glory of the right One. Here is a concise statement that you should remember when resisting the devil: Do what Jesus did!

Jesus resisted the devil by refusing to entertain the devil's lies. Then He spoke the Truth of God's Word. His response to the devil's lies was in stark contrast to Eve's response to the serpent in Genesis 3. The serpent asked her, "Did God actually say . . .?" (Genesis 3:1). She considered the serpent's argument as if it had validity and was seduced to not only eat the forbidden fruit but to give some to Adam as well. Jesus knew that the devil was the "father of lies" and that he is out to kill, maim, and destroy, and so Jesus refused to dialogue with the devil. In the account of the temptation of Jesus by the devil in Matthew 4, Jesus responded immediately by quoting Scripture which is the Truth of God's Word.

You must do as Jesus did in order to resist the devil. Do not do what the devil asks you to do even though every thought in your head and every strong emotion in your heart might be telling you to do so. Unclench your fist. Do not seek comfort or help from anyone that you know is inappropriate. Stop wasting hours deep into the night plotting revenge. Do not give in, give up, or do anything that you know you will later cause you shame, guilt, or fear. Instead, submit your heart's emotions and your mind's thoughts to God and respond righteously. Walk away. Keep your mouth shut. Do not aggravate or intensify the situation. In fact, respond biblically: turn the other cheek, if forced to go one mile then go two miles, and pray for those who persecute you.[2]

> **Do not give in, give up, or do anything that you know you will later cause you shame, guilt, or fear. Instead, submit your heart's emotions and your mind's thoughts to God and respond righteously.**

At first, resisting the devil may go against your nature. But as you continue to resist him, refuse to do what he dictates. Act on your submission of your heart and mind to God, then you will discover that the devil will flee because he has no other course of action. He can only tempt you and cannot make you do what you do not want to do. He is a coward who will run away and attempt to ambush you in a weak moment at a later time.

3. DRAW NEAR TO GOD, AND HE WILL DRAW NEAR TO YOU.

If you will move toward God, you will find that He will move toward you. God loves you so much that He sent His one and only Son to pay the penalty of your sins by dying in your place. God the

---

2 Matthew 5:39, 41, 44.

Father is eagerly seeking to be in relationship with you. God the Son rose again on the third day and intercedes for you as He is before the Father. God the Holy Spirit is the Advocate who reveals the mind of Christ to us and intercedes on our behalf. God is looking for you! You must look for God!

The question then is just how close do you really want to get to God? When you go before the Lord you will discover quickly that all of your pretense, facades, and barriers that you built and place around yourself are meaningless before Him. God sees right through them. He knew you before you were born. He knows your thoughts before you think them. He goes behind you and at the same time goes before you.

Your best course of action then is to be honest with Him and with yourself. Your "wisdom" is utter foolishness to the Lord. Your "righteousness" is like filthy rags. Acknowledge His greatness and fall at His feet. He is the Almighty. He is the Creator. You are the created. The more that you are willing to empty yourself of your pride and ego, the more space you will be available for God to fill.

The promise that God gave to King Solomon and the Children of Israel is a promise for you: "If my people who are called by my name humble themselves, and pray and seek my face and turn from their wicked ways, then I will hear from heaven and will forgive their sin and heal their land" (2 Chronicles 7:14).

Now, let's consider this from the perspective that you humbled yourself before the Lord and you are seeking Him desperately! Be encouraged that God hears your prayers, He will stand with you, and He will never leave you or give up on you! The word of God through His prophet Jeremiah is another promise for you: "You will seek me and find me when you seek me with all your heart" (Jeremiah 29:13).

This is the point in your life when you must come to God as if your life depends on it. The reality is your life does indeed depend on you finding and connecting with Him. So turn off the television, get off social networks, quit listening to any music that is not drawing you closer to God, walk away from relationships that are not Christ-centered, and get into God's Word, the Bible. That's right; open your Bible and read like your life depended on it—because it does!

Many of us in your situation have found great comfort and strength by reading aloud the Psalms as if they were our prayers to the Lord. You will be surprised at how God's Word will vocalize what you are feeling in your heart right now. In fact, every book in the Bible will resonant with your broken heart, will reveal the character of God, and will draw you close to Him. Psalm 25:16–21 is an excellent example:

> *Turn to me and be gracious to me, for I am lonely and afflicted. The troubles of my heart are enlarged; bring me out of my distresses. Consider my affliction and my trouble, and forgive all my sins. Consider how many are my foes, and with what violent hatred they hate me. Oh, guard my soul, and deliver me! Let me not be put to shame, for I take refuge in you. May integrity and uprightness preserve me, for I wait for you.*

Go near to the Lord and He will go near to you.

4. CLEANSE YOUR HANDS, YOU SINNERS,

You may feel that you are a victim and did not deserve whatsoever to get hit in the mouth by life. However, this action still requires your introspection. Did you do something that may have caused, or at least contributed to, your predicament? What could you have done differently? It is at this point that you must confess what you did, no matter how much or little it may be, and seek to restore that which was lost.

Cleansing your hands means that you will come clean before God. You will admit your past mistakes and seek His forgiveness. This action is vital to your recovery. If you hold back and refuse to be cleansed completely then you are doomed to failure.

The first step in cleansing your hands requires an honest assessment of your actions, and the inner strength to acknowledge your faults, in order to get all aspects of your situation open before God. The point is not to assign blame and therefore gain a false sense of self-worth by putting down or accusing your offender. The idea is to identify areas of your weaknesses so that you can turn them over to Jesus, learn to act rightly, and to ensure that the past is not repeated.

> **Cleansing your hands means that you will come clean before God. You will admit your past mistakes and seek His forgiveness. This action is vital to your recovery.**

Was there any truth to what your offender said? What did you do, if anything, that led to your offender's action or reaction to you? If you could rewind the story of your life, what would you do over? What should you learn from this incident so that it will not be repeated? These are the types of questions that you should ask yourself. I encourage you strongly to interact with a trusted counselor who knows how to touch the heart of God. Such an individual can be used by the Lord to sift through what is truth and falsehood, what is real and imagined, and then direct you to an evaluation through the filter of God's Word.

Once you have identified your growth points, repent! Repenting does not mean that you say only that you are sorry. Repentance means that you admit your wrong actions or thoughts, you apologize to God, make amends to the one you offended, and then act rightly.

As an example, let's say that you were fired from your work. You were humiliated by that action and you now face a financial crisis: you have a family to feed and a mortgage to meet. It might make you feel good to speak badly of your boss and detail his wrongdoings, but that feeling is temporary at best. A better action would be to consider the reasons why you were released from your job, make amends, and diligently act in a manner that will benefit your company. Should you be unable to return to your former place of employment, this may determine whether a new company will hire you. Remember that the only way to regain credibility is for your actions to represent your words.

As you are cleansing your hands by assessing honestly your situation and by repenting, you must remember that you are accountable for your actions only. My counselor told me, "Mark, you can eat only your piece of the pie of responsibility!" While there is truth to the fact my actions caused a reaction, I cannot take full responsibility for the response by my offender for that is something only the offender can do. However, I am accountable for my actions and reactions, no matter what is done to me, just as my offender is responsible for his or her actions and reactions. This was a difficult lesson for me to learn!

Note: this does not apply to children, as they do not have the emotional maturity to process the situation, nor to act and respond appropriately. Jesus had harsh words for one who causes a little one who believes in Him to sin as seen in Matthew 18:5–6.

We can take responsibility for our actions alone. An example of this is when the spouse who stayed thinks that if only he or she had done this better or said that or had not reacted so strongly that the wife or husband would not have turned to an affair and then separated and then divorced. We can waste so much emotional energy taking blame for the actions of others. In fact, we can cleanse only our hands, not the hands of others. However, what we can do is to pray for our offender, release him or her to the Lord, and move forward by seeking the Lord and acting rightly.

5. AND PURIFY YOUR HEARTS, YOU DOUBLE-MINDED.

Purifying your heart is a key defensive tactic because it requires that you deal with your emotions and motives which are issues of your heart. While time may pass from the actual incident, the battle you face continually is a battle in your heart and mind. You may never get over what happened to you but you can learn to manage it by responding appropriately to the offense and then live in freedom.

Your fight now is to overcome the mind games in the battlefield in your mind. If you allow your emotions to be released unabated or seek to balance the scales of justice by your own actions, then you are doomed for even more pain and suffering. The truth is that instead of moving forward in victory, such actions will impede your defensive strategy, and you will be hit again and again before you can counter-attack.

You will be tempted strongly to get revenge on the one who hurt you and to respond to the pain by reciprocating with intensity. You may play mind games by convincing yourself that you will be justified in doing so. But the proper response to the one who caused you great pain is not to get revenge by responding in the way your offender hurt you. If you do, you will be trapped in an endless downward spiral of deceit and vendettas, which will ultimately result in personal destruction. This is most definitely a "lose-lose" proposition.

If you seek revenge on your offender, then there are two outcomes. First, the one who hurt you will move from being your offender to being your adversary. When you face your offender, then you are positioned to be the victim at some level. But when you face your adversary you move dangerously close to being judge, jury, and executioner, and you move from being the victim to being the offender. Once you toss aside the boundaries of right and wrong in order to get your revenge, you crossed a line morally, and to regain your moral compass is very difficult, if not impossible.

The second outcome of taking justice into your own hands is you will respond to your offender with the same behavior that caused you pain. Do you really want to live and function in the depths of suffering where you were taken? When we were children, we were taught that "two wrongs do not make a right," and that wisdom certainly applies here. Your hope of recovery does not lie in lowering yourself to the level of your offender, but in following the teachings of Jesus Christ and rising above the fray. This is the move, the only move, that will allow you to regain your sense of balance and to find hope and peace again.

> **When you face your adversary you move dangerously close to being judge, jury, and executioner, and you move from being the victim to being the offender.**

Revisiting in your mind over and over the episodes of your pain deep into the night not only wastes your emotional energy and causes you to lose sleep, but it is an unproductive exercise that offers no positive outcome. You cannot function rightly when you are outwardly living by the rules of being a good Christian, while inwardly your heart and your mind are plotting revenge. This is an example of being double-minded. Look in a mirror right now and see who is looking back at you. The person you see is the only one you are fooling. That person is you.

A positive response is to admit what you are feeling, allow yourself to feel that way for a time, and if possible, express your emotions and motives to your trusted Christian counselor. Ask the Lord to help you gain control of your emotions and your motives. Then, focus your heart and your mind on a proper response from God's Word; that which is righteous and true. Release these thoughts to the Lord and allow Him to do what He does best. He will bring you peace in the midst of life's storm. He will balance the scales of justice according to His plan and time.

I know from experience that purifying your heart after getting knockout blow can be extremely difficult. My suggestion is that you address the issue one emotional attack at a time. The Lord will give you the strength to fight the feelings to lash back by developing your self-control and by replacing those feelings with thoughts and actions that will honor Him.

6. BE WRETCHED (GRIEVE, NIV)

The Book of James tells us that we are to be wretched, that is to grieve about what happened to us. Grieving, to me, is an inward adjustment to a traumatic loss. As we have stated, the loss is like being punched in the mouth by life. Relationships are betrayed, covenants and contracts are broken, our lives are impacted by natural disasters or illness and the loss of your job are all examples of traumatic events that bring disaster to our lives.

Such loss demands an adjustment on our part. We cannot just collect the remnants of our lives and live as if nothing happened. You can try to ignore the need to make this adjustment or try to fill the void with relationships, activities, or whatever brings you pleasure. At the end of the day such actions are postponing the inevitable encounter with the loss. A vital step in re-creating or rebuilding our lives is to admit that the trauma occurred and deal with it in a healthy manner.

The grieving process is inward in that it involves the battlefield of our heart and mind. Your emotions and your will are influenced by the trauma and you are tempted to function outside the boundaries of your belief system. These are the moments that you must gain control of your heart and mind by examining your situation and future behaviors not through the events that led to the trauma, but through the filter of your relationship with the Lord.

The bottom line is that you must allow yourself to grieve! One reason is grieving your loss is actually a step toward recovery. You must deal with the ashes of your life before you can rebuild. Another reason is if you do not allow yourself to grieve properly, then at some point in your life your emotions and your intellect will express your internal pain in ways that will either hurt those around you or bring you more pain. For example, one day one of your children will do something that requires your parental response but instead of doing so in a manner befitting their behavior you respond with fiery anger. This hurts the very one you love and breaks down that relationship. You are not responding rightly to the child, but you allow their behavior to be a trigger that sparks your anger simmering just below the surface of your emotions. It will be best for you in the long term to deal with your grief now so that you can deal with it appropriately, rather than to avoid the grief and have

If you do not allow yourself to grieve properly, then at some point in your life your emotions and your intellect will express your internal pain in ways that will either hurt those around you or bring you more pain.

it seep out in ways that cause more pain and possible embarrassment.

We who were raised in first world nations often lack the background and knowledge of the benefits of grieving or even how to grieve. We tend to avoid grieving at all costs, like it is a deadly disease. We are much better at celebrating our victories and shouting "we're number one" than we are standing with a defeated one who is suffering in solitude.

Your pain hurts deeply. I do not deny what happened to you or the consequences that it has on your life. You must not deny this either! I believe that the Book of James directs us to grieve because grieving helps us to acknowledge the events that knocked us down. Also, it forces us to assess honestly our feelings and pain, and serves as a vital step to recovery once we interact with it genuinely.

Counselors tell us that there are at least five stages of grief: denial, anger, bargaining, depression, and acceptance. You need to discuss these stages with your counselor so you can understand your current mental, emotional, and spiritual state, then respond appropriately. I am not a trained counselor; however, I will make some comments about the grieving process that you should address.

First, the stages of the grieving process are not necessarily experienced in sequential order. Rather than moving from denial to anger to bargaining, you will discover that the stages come to you like ocean waves onto a beach. Sometimes, the wave will bring one stage, while at other times the waves will bring a stage that you did not expect. So do not be discouraged that just when you feel that you have overcome denial and moved on to anger, another wave of denial will hit you. The evil one will lie to you and attempt to cause you to doubt that you are making progress in your recovery. He wants to lead you to negative self-talk and question whether or not your responses are bringing the desired result. Doubt will lead to discouragement, discouragement leads to quitting, and quitting results in defeat. Just remember that often the recovery process is addressed one layer at a time, rather than all at once.

The encouraging aspect of the randomness of the waves of grief is that when you respond appropriately—that is, in a manner that honors Christ—then you will discover that the waves start to arrive in decreasing intensity and frequency. My advice to you is that rather than being discouraged by the reappearance of a grief stage, be encouraged that you know now how to respond in a Christ-like manner when it does arrive. This will allow you to pave new roads of responses rather than being trapped in the old ruts of despair.

The saying, "time heals all wounds," implies that somehow the turning of the calendar will equip you to regain your life balance and move forward. There may be some wisdom in the saying for there are events in life that are best left behind in our past. But over time, your continual proper response to each grief wave will bring healing as you learn new life skills to manage grief and to use those events of the past to your advantage. You will discover also as you respond in a healthy manner that the intensity of the waves will diminish, as I mentioned before. The initial waves will knock you down like a tsunami. But as you learn to lean on the Lord and to respond biblically, you will reduce the impact of the waves dramatically until you render them meaningless.

Second, if you want to stand, you must acknowledge the stage you are experiencing and act accordingly. For example, when you are angry, then allow yourself to be angry. But as the Bible says, "in your anger do not sin" (Ephesians 4:26, NIV). You might be tempted to feel guilty for being angry, but that will only accentuate the problem. Acknowledge the anger instead, share your feelings with your counselor or those in your inner circle, and seek to respond biblically. Any attempt to ignore or deny the stage you are in will only increase the difficulty.

Third, your attempts to dull the pain, reduce the pain, or ignore that pain may bring an immediate relief, but the pain will return and will become exponentially worse. You can go all over town and speak badly of the one who hurt you and feel good about yourself while you do it. But that will not bring healing to your pain or revenge to the one who hurt you. You can fill your life will activity and even sensual pleasures, but in doing so you will create only more problems. The pain will return and return with increased intensity. The best response is to address your pain directly and properly. In the short term, it will seem to bring more pain, but it will be a significant step toward healing.

> **You were punched in the mouth by life and are now in a season of weakness. This is the exact moment that you must hold strong to your relationship with Jesus Christ and allow Him to have control.**

Fourth, if you seek to address your grief stage in a healthy manner—a biblical manner—then you will discover that in God's time, the season will change and you will be open to God's healing. When we turn our hearts to the Lord in our season of brokenness, we open a door for Him to enter and allow His strength to comfort and guide us in our weakness. You were punched in the mouth by life and are now in a season of weakness. This is the exact moment that you must hold strong to your relationship with Jesus Christ and allow Him to have control. The apostle Paul did this and wrote, "For when I am weak, then I am strong" (2 Corinthians 12:10). You will discover that the Lord will be your strength. As you draw closer to the Lord in your weakness, you will discover that He will give you His strength. This positions you to build a new foundation of strength and hope in Christ for a clear and bright future.

If you want to stand one day soon, then you must allow yourself a season of grieving the wrong that was done to you. You cannot walk away unscathed. You must address the pain, dig deeply into your heart and mind, and seek to learn to rebuild in a manner that honors Christ. When you do, you will be standing and living as an overcomer.

7. MOURN

It is natural that mourning will follow grief. Mourning is an outward adjustment to a traumatic loss. It is passionate grief that cannot be hidden. When you mourn, you are expressing outwardly your inner grieving. Such a public expression will allow your friends and coworkers to know your situation and to respond in a manner that is appropriate, at least culturally. For example, when you suffer the death of a loved one, your public mourning will be a signal to your coworkers that you

> **It is important to your spiritual, emotional, and even physical health to grieve and to mourn. Most importantly, you must remember that God sees you in these times and He has not forgotten you.**

are not at your best, that your work may decline for a season, and that you will need time away from work to deal appropriately with your loss.

While we each may mourn in different ways and for varied lengths of time, it is important to your spiritual, emotional, and even physical health to grieve and to mourn. Most importantly, you must remember that God sees you in these times and He has not forgotten you. In fact, it is in these moments that you will discover His presence will be strongest in your heart.

I find it odd that a frequent response by one who was abandoned in a relationship is to quickly enter into a new relationship as if to show the world that "all is well!" and that "life goes on!" without hesitation. In reality, what is needed is a time to withdraw for introspection and time with the Lord for healing and instruction. Jumping into a new relationship or life situation before one is emotionally and spiritually prepared can often create new problems and highlight weaknesses. This can be unsettling for your children as well. They need time to mourn and to express their feelings over the relationship loss. Bringing a new person into the family prematurely can cause children to withdraw and feel even more anger over the situation.

I feel it important that you express your feelings of mourning only to your inner circle of friends. Others can know that you are mourning, but they do not need to be subjected to hearing the details of what is going on in your heart and life. The Lord will bring people into your life who can walk with you through this season. But please note that not everyone can do this. Be willing to forgive your friends who cannot walk with you as they may not be equipped emotionally or spiritually to be of assistance. While they may not interact with you regularly, they will continue to pray God's blessing for you and be there when you move to a new season of life.

You are the only one who can know how long you should mourn. A general rule is that the deeper the loss, the longer the mourning period. Mourning is a season you must experience, but it is not where you will live the rest of your life. Like grieving, you must mourn as part of your recovery, but at some point you must accept the situation, allow the Lord to bring healing, and move forward with your life. The constant pain you feel in your heart will lessen. You will eventually exhale and breathe again. The Lord will help you rebuild.

8. WEEP (WAIL, NIV)

Society in first world nations no longer allow mourners to wail publicly unless they are at a funeral service. But wailing is a vital step in your recovery process. Wailing is an audible expression of one's grief and mourning. There is therapeutic value in vocalizing the pain in your heart.

You may not have a personality that is demonstrative in public. That is not a problem. But even you must allow yourself time to express completely your pain and to give the entirety of it to God. When you are in your private time before the Lord, you are allowed to shout, to cry, to sob, to moan; whatever you want. God is big enough to handle your raw emotions and even your raw language. The point is for you to be open before God and to pour the entirety of your being before Him. Let it all out before God and do not hold back!

Those who wailed in biblical times sobbed openly, tore their clothes, wore sackcloth and ashes, fasted, and sometimes even cut their beards. This was an outward express of their inner pain. The benefit was that the one doing the wailing was able to deal completely with the inner turmoil.

As stated with previous behaviors, your emotions will be expressed one way or another, so it is best to do so when you have self-control rather than to allow your emotions to spew onto others in inappropriate ways and times.

So go ahead and wail! Tell God how you really feel! But when you are done doing so, do not remain in that stage. Once your expression is complete, even to the point of exhaustion, get up, wash yourself, and in all sincerity declare, "May the name of the

Lord be praised" (Job 1:21, NIV) and pray, "Father, . . . not my will, but yours be done" (Luke 23:42).

9. LET YOUR LAUGHTER BE TURNED TO MOURNING AND YOUR JOY TO GLOOM.

Recently, I witnessed a man respond to a loss of relationship by acting as if he had recovered completely in just a short period of time. He was acting like "a man" and "a man cuts his losses and moves forward." My heart was saddened for him because he was far from being healed, and seemed to be in denial. I prayed that he would allow himself to find strength in the Lord.

Take seriously what happened to you. Your attempts to ignore the offense against you, to pretend that it did not bother you, or to deny that it happened will only accentuate the pain. You will respond to the pain eventually, and if you are not careful, you may divert your anger onto someone undeserving of your attacks and do collateral damage to innocent people and loved ones. Instead, you must acknowledge the pain, go through the healing process, and get on the road to recovery.

Ecclesiastes 3:1 tells us that "there is a time for everything, and a season for every activity under heaven." There is even "a time to weep, and a time to laugh; a time to mourn, and a time to dance" (Ecclesiastes 3:4). You are in a season where it is time to mourn and to be in gloom. Take this season seriously and act biblically.

10. HUMBLE YOURSELVES BEFORE THE LORD, AND HE WILL EXALT YOU.

If you empty yourself and give the entirety of your being over to the Lord, you will discover that He is faithful and He will lift you up in due time. The longer that you fight your pain, fight your offender, and even blame God, then the longer you will live under the cloud of defeat. The sooner that you humble yourself completely, the sooner you will be to allowing the healing hand of the Holy Spirit to penetrate to the core of your being and to re-create you into the person He destined you to be.

You have been hurt and possibly broken. But you have the responsibility and the ability to respond. The more that you attempt to rebuild on your own, the more you will flounder in weakness. However, the more that you humble yourself before the Lord and follow diligently after Him, then the more you will rebuild and be on the road to recovery. This is your choice and your choice alone.

11. DO NOT SPEAK EVIL AGAINST ONE ANOTHER, BROTHERS.

We discussed this already, but it must be emphasized again. It will not benefit you in the long term, it does not endear you to your friends, and it does not honor the Lord to slander, berate, denigrate, or demean your offender to others. Yes, you can express your honest feelings to those in your inner circle and that is appropriate for a time. But slandering your offender before others will cause further pain and division and is not becoming of you or those you represent—especially the Lord. There is nothing good that comes from you slandering your offender!

> The more that you humble yourself before the Lord and follow diligently after Him, then the more you will rebuild and be on the road to recovery. This is your choice and your choice alone.

James' directive is especially invaluable when applied to those in your home. Your children hear your words, feel your pain, and take your emotions personally. While you cannot change what happened to you, your response will bring either comfort and healing into your home or be like a cancer or poison. When your children take on your anger, then their emotion and spiritual growth is stunted and is expressed negatively in ways such as poor self-image, lack of academic drive, and even deviant behavior. It will be you then who perpetuates life's punch in your mouth to the next generation. So it must be you who takes responsibility and declares that while life may have punched you, it will not impact your children.

If you insist on slandering your offender, then you are allowing the offender to dictate your life. Your friends will grow tired of hearing your constant counter-attacks and will soon avoid you altogether. Such speech will become tiresome and serve only to ruin your reputation. So when you feel like saying something negative about your offender to others—and those feelings will be strong—you must exhibit self-control and refuse to slander. The old adage applies: "If you don't have anything nice to say, don't say anything at all."

Once you determine to remain silent, remind yourself that the Lord knows exactly what happened and who is at fault. It is the Lord alone who will balance the scales of justice and it is He who will give each of us what we deserve. Let the Lord get your revenge. Rather than insisting on revealing the faults of your offender, turn your offender over to the Lord, and ask Him to help you keep your heart pure and righteous. When you do this, you will gain a freedom that only the Lord can give. You will be tied to the past no longer and will then be positioned to move forward in victory. This is your choice and your choice alone.

The first response to being knocked down by life is to do whatever you can to ensure that you will not be knocked down again. Thankfully, the passage from James teaches you a classic defensive strategy that will protect you and make you stronger in the long run. Now, it is time to consider offensive strategy. It is time to fight back! In the coming chapter, you will learn the apostle Paul's strategy to winning life's battles. He will give you ten "Victory Actions" that you can apply to your life. Are you ready to fight back? Are you ready to win?

FOR YOU TO CONSIDER

1. Pray Psalm 139:23–24 aloud right now.

2. List three actions and thoughts that you should apply to your life in order to resist the devil.

3. What two actions must you take to draw near to God?

4. What responsibility, if any, must you take for your current situation?

5. Ask the Lord to help you to gain control of your emotions and motives instead of wasting emotional energy seeking revenge.

6. How did you deal with grief in the past? How should you deal with it after reading this chapter?

7.   What can you do to mourn?

8.   Get alone and express your emotions to God. Remember to write down your feeling in a journal. You may want to express yourself verbally. Release your feelings and then create a statement of praise to the Lord.

9.   Share the three actions that show you are taking seriously your current situation.

10. Ask the Lord to take control of your heart, mind, and emotions.

11. Determine in your heart not to slander your offender.

SCRIPTURE FOR YOU TO PRAY TODAY

"Oh, guard my soul, and deliver me! Let me not be put to shame, for I take refuge in you. May integrity and uprightness preserve me, for I wait for you" (Psalm 25:20–21).

What is the Lord saying to you right now?

3

VICTORY ACTIONS

We have discussed already the idea that when we get knocked down, we must get off the canvas of life, regain our sense of balance, and live again. The passage in James provided us with an effective strategy to defend ourselves so that we will not be hit again. Now, it is time to counter-attack. It is time to look our opponent in the eye and punch him in the mouth! The moment of victory that has been your focus since you were wounded has arrived now. The winning strategy that will put you back on the road to fulfilling your God-given destiny is probably not quite what you envisioned.

In the Book of Ephesians, the apostle Paul presented powerfully the deity of our Lord Jesus Christ and then detailed how we, as ones who call ourselves Christians, ought to live in light of our relationship with Him. Paul wrote that believers should throw off the old nature and put on the new self. We are to be imitators of God. Wives and husbands should love and respect one another. Children and parents should get along. Workers and masters must realize that they are all accountable to God for their behavior. This wonderful book encourages us to be in harmony with others. This is amazing material that we should apply to our lives in every relationship.

It fascinates me that the final chapter encourages us to "be strong in the Lord and in the strength of his might" (Ephesians 6:10). Paul knew that when we are living a righteous life that honors Christ, the devil will fight back. When we live rightly our life story will not end with "and they lived happily ever after," without challenges. Attacks are going to happen! Attacks are unavoidable! The devil will not sit idly by while believers are growing closer to the Lord by living in harmony with each other. He will launch his counter-attack and throw all of his energies and resources into destroying God's children. But we are not captive to the devil's schemes. We can live in freedom that comes only from Jesus Christ.

Are you ready to go on the offensive and feel the vibrancy of a fulfilled life? Are you ready to move forward in victory?

No longer will you be suffocated by the hopelessness of your situation. You can be released from the bonds of helplessness and regain your sense of hope. You can rebuild your life and move into a season of a positive sense of self-worth, productivity, and yes, even genuine joy. In the remainder of our journey together, we will examine closely Paul's strategy to winning life's battles that will lead you to give a biblical response when life knocks you down. He encouraged us to "be strong in the Lord and in his mighty power" and defined that phrase with ten specific, time-tested, and biblical responses—Victory Actions—that you must embrace whole-heartedly to stand firm and live a life of victory. Are you ready to go on the offensive and feel the vibrancy of a fulfilling life? Are you ready to move forward in victory?

VICTORY ACTION 1

PUT ON
THE WHOLE ARMOR OF GOD
LIVE BY GOD'S RULES

"Finally, be strong in the Lord and in the strength of his might. Put on the whole armor of God, that you may be able to stand against the schemes of the devil. For we do not wrestle against flesh and blood, but against the rulers, against the authorities, against the cosmic powers over this present darkness, against the spiritual forces of evil in the heavenly places."

EPHESIANS 6:10–12

"Be sober-minded; be watchful. Your adversary the devil prowls around like a roaring lion, seeking someone to devour. Resist him, firm in your faith, knowing that the same kinds

of suffering are being experienced by your
brotherhood throughout the world."

1 PETER 5:8-9

"Finally, brothers, whatever is true, whatever is
honorable, whatever is just, whatever is pure,
whatever is lovely, whatever is commendable,
if there is any excellence, if there is anything
worthy of praise, think about these things."

PHILIPPIANS 4:8

Champ started round four with a rapid flurry of jabs that stunned Destroyer. But he recovered quickly with a powerful left hook that snapped back Champ's head and drove him deep into the ropes. Destroyer moved forward with steely determination and attacked with such raw power that I figured he was trying to end the fight right then and there. It was all Champ could do to lift his fists in front of his own face in a defensive survival posture and pray that the nightmare would end. Destroyer pounded and pounded into Champ's midsection, trying to break his ribs and knock the wind from him. This fight was going to be over soon.

As the pounding continued mercilessly, Champ surprised me once again. When Destroyer positioned himself for the knockout *blow, Champ peeked slyly over his gloves to see what his opponent was doing. That quick glance was the key to his strategy! He was doing the old "rope a dope."*

My mind shot back to 1974 when I was a kid and woke up at 3 am to watch "The Rumble in the Jungle" with my Dad. That night Muhammad Ali fought George Forman in Zaire for the Heavyweight Championship of the world. Champ was employing Ali's tactics of allowing the bigger and stronger opponent to throw hay-makers right and left while he leaned on the ropes in a defensive stance. Ali saved himself from being knocked out while in the process sapping the strength of the aggressor. While the beating inflicted upon Champ was painful, no doubt, he was able to deflect the blows with his arms and avoid a knockout punch to his face.

The strategy worked perfectly in the middle rounds. As Destroyer kept pounding you could see his frustration increasing. He attacked in every way possible, but each assault resulted in nothing but glancing blows. When the bell sounded to end the sixth round, Destroyer collapsed in his corner in total exhaustion. Champ stood firm in the ring, survived his opponent's best shots, and knew that his victory was imminent.

The first step to "be strong in the Lord and in the strength of his might" (Ephesians 6:10) is to consider being equipped spiritually to fight the evil one as a warrior is equipped in battle. While the armor is vitally important, we will not focus on the armor itself, but rather, on what it represents. Our new responses to our personal dramas will be focused on the whole armor of God, standing firm, truth, righteousness, peace, faith, hope that comes from our salvation, the Word of God, prayer in the Spirit, and praying for God's people. These are the actions that empower us to "be strong in the Lord and in the strength of his might." These are the actions that will guarantee victory!

Some of the Victory Actions may come more easily for you than others, but all of them must be addressed. The hope and victory that you crave are found in living as Jesus lived. And most importantly, He will join you in this battle and bring victory!

> **Putting on the whole armor of God means that you will respond in the way that He directs, trusting in Him completely, seeking His desired outcomes, and leaving your future in His hands . . . It must be God's way or no way; either you are in all the way or not at all.**

Paul's strategy to winning life's battles begins with Victory Action 1: Put on the Whole Armor of God. Paul directed us in no uncertain terms to "put on the whole armor of God so that you can take your stand against the schemes of the devil" (Ephesians 6:11). Putting on the whole armor of God means that you will respond in the way that He directs, trusting in Him completely, seeking His desired outcomes, and leaving your future in His hands. Your heart and will must be in this completely or you are doomed to an endless cycle of frustration and despair like Sisyphus (mentioned in chapter 1). It must be God's way or no way; either you are in all the way or not at all.

If we were sitting across a table right now, I would stop and ask you, "Are you willing to live and fight by God's rules and not by your rules?" If you are ready to declare to the Lord, "not my will but yours be done," then you are ready to implement Victory Action 1 and move confidently in Paul's winning strategy. If you want to hang on to your pain, live as a victim, and respond according to the way your old nature is screaming in your ear to respond (for example, with revenge), then you are not ready to move forward in victory. Truthfully, if this latter description characterizes your heart, then you may not be ready yet to move forward in victory. Your path for vindication will lead to more pain, more hurt, and an immense amount of collateral damage to your family and friends.

Let's consider briefly the Old Testament character named Job and place him in our contemporary context. Job was a man who had it all: wife, children, wealth beyond imagination, respect, admiration. He was living the good life! "This man was the greatest of all the people of the east" (Job 1:3). Suddenly, and for no reason known to him, life hit him smack in the mouth and laid him out on the canvas. He lost everything! All of his children died, his financial empire was destroyed overnight, his respect from others turned to disdain, and he had to endure ridicule from lesser men.

This was the most challenging battle in Job's life for his character was being tested. Would he continue to love God because God was worthy, or would he curse God and die because God had seemingly turned His back on him?

Now, you are in Job's position and you must decide how you will respond to the one who hurt you. By whose rules will you fight? Some people whose lives are ripped apart by adultery respond by getting into a new relationship immediately with someone younger or wealthier or more beautiful just to show the offending spouse, "Who needs you? I am better off without you!" This attempt to rebuild quickly and to a seemingly better life is portrayed by our old nature as an appropriate response and one that will elevate your self-worth and diminish the self-worth and actions of your offender.

Some trapped in this nightmare will seek revenge and respond with the attitude of "you hurt me, but I will hurt you more!" When you employ this strategy, you are following the schemes of the devil by lowering yourself to the mind-set and tactics of your offender. You are out of control because you are driven by your offender instead of living in freedom.

You may feel justified by exhibiting your anger because of the way you were treated by the one you can see and the one you can hurt. While this may bring you temporary joy, you will soon discover that your quest for revenge in fact makes matters worse. You are acting in a manner that was produced from your old nature, the one you had before you met Christ, that baits you into fighting by the rules of your spiritual adversary. When you do this, you lose.

> **The battle in which you are engaged will not be won by overpowering your adversary, but only by aligning your heart and mind strategically with Christ Jesus. Now is the exact time for you to throw off the response devices given to you by your old nature. Now is the exact time for you to put on the whole armor of God.**

The battle in which you are engaged will not be won by overpowering your adversary, but only by aligning your heart and mind strategically with Christ Jesus. Now is the exact time for you to throw off the response devices given to you by your old nature. Now is the exact time for you to put on the whole armor of God. Paul wrote that you put on the whole armor and not part of the armor or the part of the armor that you like or even the part of the armor that you understand. You are to put on the armor in its entirety. You must take off the armor of your old nature completely or there will not be room for the whole armor of God.

Your attempts to rebuild your life and recover your self-worth and the "glory" of your former life may bring results temporarily, but it will prove fleeting because your new house is built on sand and not on the rock.[1] But if you choose to follow Jesus, He will re-create your life on solid rock, and then you will be equipped to withstand the raging storms of life.

The prerequisites for our Victory Action 1 are that you must want to stand (as discussed in Chapter 1) and you must embrace your pain and regain your sense of balance (as discussed in Chapter 2). Now, you must rediscover Jesus and respond to being hit in the mouth by living in a manner that serves and honors Him.

You must live now by Jesus' rules! Remember Matthew 11:28–30:

> *"Come to me, all you who labor and are heavy laden, and I will give you rest. Take my yoke upon you, and learn from me, for I am gentle and lowly in heart, and you will find rest for your souls. For my yoke is easy and my burden is light."*

It is in the most difficult circumstances of life that you must rededicate yourself unequivocally to the Master. Put on the yoke of Christ and learn to "Love your enemies, do good to those who hate you, bless those who curse you, pray for those who abuse you" (Luke 6:27–28). Learn to "Judge not, and you will not be judged. Condemn not, and you will not be condemned; forgive, and you will be forgiven; give, and it will be given to you. Good measure, pressed down, shaken together, running over, will be put into your lap. For with the measure you use, it will be measured back to you"

---

1 Matthew 7:24–27.

(Luke 6:37–38).

Fighting by Jesus' rules does not come naturally to us, especially in those seasons of intense hurt. It may go against your old nature to not retaliate with words or actions, but you must remember that you are driven no longer by your old nature! You are a new creation in Christ Jesus and His ways of responding will get you through this trial.

If you take on the yoke of Jesus you will learn to live in the freedom of His presence in your life and be freed from the enslavement of your adversary. If you follow Christ wholeheartedly, He will balance the scales of justice, He will clear your name, He will rebuild your life, and He will bring you blessing. He will take that which was meant to harm you and turn it into good. He will take you in your weakness, get you on your feet again, and make you stronger as you follow Him. He will refocus your season of pain and despair to be one of refinement and character building as you trust in Him.

Our friend, Job, could have been mad at God, tried to gain revenge on those who attacked him during his weakness, and attempted to regain his empire by all means possible. Instead, he chose to remain faithful to the Lord even though he did not understand the reason for his trials. The Bible recorded Job's response to being hit in the mouth by life in Job 1:21–22, "'Naked I came from my mother's womb, and naked shall I return. The Lord gave, and the Lord has taken away; blessed be the name of the Lord.' In all this Job did not sin or charge God with wrong." The ultimate outcome of Job's season of tribulation was that he discovered the greatness of God. God revealed His character to Job and "blessed the latter days of Job more than his beginning" (Job 42:12). I pray that you and I will respond in the same manner for this allows us to put on the whole armor of God.

The reason that you are to put on the whole armor of God is

so you will be equipped to take your stand against the devil. In Ephesians 6, Paul directed us to "stand against," "stand your ground" (NIV), and "stand firm" in response to the devil. It is only when you wear the whole armor of God that you will be prepared and equipped to withstand the spiritual attacks of the evil one. Let me rephrase this: the winning strategy to rebuilding your life starts with living God's way. It brings a guarantee of victory. Putting on the whole armor of

The ultimate cause for your pain and suffering is not the adversary you see, but rather, it is the puppet master behind the curtain who is deviously manipulating humanity: he is the devil.

God empowers you to stand firm against the devil and guarantees that you will see victory for the following reasons:

1. GOD'S ARMOR WINS ALL SPIRITUAL BATTLES.

The ultimate cause for your pain and suffering is not the adversary you see, but rather, it is the puppet master behind the curtain who is deviously manipulating humanity: he is the devil. Paul wrote,

> "For we do not wrestle against flesh and blood, but against the rulers, against the authorities, against the cosmic powers over this present darkness, against the spiritual forces of evil in the heavenly places. Therefore take up the whole armor of God, that you may be able to withstand in the evil day, and having done all, to stand firm" (Ephesians 6:12–13).

You know full and well that Jesus Christ conquered sin by His death on the cross and that He conquered death by His resurrection on the third day. There is no power greater than Jesus Christ. He rules and reigns forever! It's like this, when you are wearing the whole armor of God, then you are wearing the jersey with the word "VICTORY!" emblazoned on the front. The devil's only hope of defeating you is for you to throw off that jersey and fight him on his terms and according to his rules. It is because of what Jesus did for you that you are no longer forced to stoop to the enemy's level. Instead, all you have to do is to wear the whole armor of God and stand firm. God will fight your battle for you!

2. GOD'S ARMOR EXPOSES THE DEVIL'S TRUE IDENTITY.

It is interesting to me that you can be in the deepest, darkest cave in the world and be completely disoriented and lost. But the moment that you shine a light, no matter how small that light may be, hope returns and you can discover how you relate to your surroundings. Light changes everything! Jesus is the Light of the world. When you focus on Him, your life has meaning and purpose.

If you will focus on Jesus, you will view your life in a completely different way. You will see that Jesus is still in control.

When you suffered a blow and fell face down on the canvas of life, you had the wind knocked out of you. Hope evaporated, lies that were told to you seemed viable, and you felt isolated and exposed. But if you will focus on Jesus, you will view your life in a completely different way. You will see that Jesus is still in control. As you put on the whole armor of God and encounter the enemy in God's strength, you will discover the identity of the devil. He is a thief and a liar. When you stand firm against him in this manner, you will discover, as we discussed earlier in James 4:7, "Submit yourselves therefore to God. Resist the devil, and he will flee from you." Submission is putting on the whole armor of God. Standing firm is resisting the devil. The evil one then will be exposed and he will run away!

Like Champ in our fictional boxing story who used the "rope a dope" tactic, you must learn to stand firm. Standing firm in a manner that honors our Lord will cause the enemy to sap his strength, to quit, and to run away.

3. GOD'S ARMOR BRINGS GLORY TO GOD.

One of my favorite childhood stories was that of David and Goliath. It was awesome how a youth could defeat a powerful giant! Truly, this was a miracle that only God could provide. There is one element of that story that I learned later in life. David rejected wearing King Saul's armor because it did not fit him. But the reason King Saul wanted David to wear his armor, I believe, was twofold. First, the King wanted to send his soldier into battle being as best equipped as possible. No one had armor and a sword better than King Saul. Second, if a miracle did occur and David did defeat the giant, then King Saul could claim the victory—or at least a major share in the victory—because David was wearing the King's armor.

Our God is so great that He shares credit with no one! There is no one equal to God and worthy of sharing His glory. When you wear the whole armor of God, you show the devil that you battle in God's authority, in God's power, with God on your side, and for God's glory.

Jesus taught us not to engage the devil by our own power in Matthew 10:28, "Do not fear those who kill the body but cannot kill the soul. Rather fear him who can destroy both soul and body in hell." Instead, when we stand on God's side, we can stand firm. Paul wrote in Romans 8:31, "What then shall we say to these things? If God is for us, who can be against us?"

4. GOD'S ARMOR UNITES YOU WITH OTHERS WHO ARE WEARING THAT SAME ARMOR.

You are not standing alone for you are not the only one recovering from being knocked down by life. Like-minded people with a kindred spirit are following diligently after God and are responding to being hit in the mouth by taking a biblical offensive strategy.

An amazing story of God's power is told in 1 Kings 18–19, when the prophet Elijah encountered the prophets of Baal. He stood alone in front of his king and the king's false prophets, all in effort to stand firm for God and against the evil one. God brought a mighty victory that day, but it was so traumatic that Elijah was forced to run for his life when threatened by Queen Jezebel. Elijah ran himself to the point of exhaustion and hid in a cave, fearful and depressed. His conversation with God sounded much like conversations you and I have had when we were in the midst of our bleakest moment. "I have been very zealous for the Lord, the God of hosts. For the people of Israel have forsaken your covenant, thrown down your altars, and killed your prophets with the sword. I, even I only, am left, and they seek my life, to take it away" (1 Kings 19:10).

Does this sound familiar? You feel isolated. You feel that you were walking rightly with the Lord, then life blindsided you and almost knocked you out. You believe that no one had endured your tragedy or your shame of being a failure. These feelings are not from the Lord, and in fact, come from the devil.

The Lord replied to Elijah by giving him an action plan and revealing what would happen in the immediate future. Then the Lord said, "'Yet I will leave seven thousand in Israel, all the knees that have not bowed down to Baal, and every mouth that has not kissed him" (1 Kings 19:18). This is truth for you as well! There are thousands of believers who are wearing the whole armor of God and standing firm against the devil. Find these people! Stand with these people for they are your friends. You will discover that you are not alone, that you are not the first one to experience such a trial, and that others who followed God now walk in victory. This will be your story too, if you respond in the same manner.

5. GOD'S ARMOR SHOWS THAT YOU LOVE GOD MORE THAN LIFE ITSELF.

When you wear the whole armor of God you declare that you are on God's side and that you will stand firm regardless of the outcome. In Daniel 3, we read of the three Hebrew young men who faced immediate death as a consequence of their refusal to bow to anyone except the True God. They stood firm before the most powerful man of their day and declared that God would rescue them. They said, "But if not, be it known to you, O king, that we will not serve your gods or worship the golden image that you have set up" (Daniel 3:18).

> You will discover that you are not alone, that you are not the first one to experience such a trial, and that others who followed God now walk in victory. This will be your story too, if you respond in the same manner.

When you love God more than life itself, then you are standing firm against the evil one and you are on the road to victory. Revelation 12:11 puts it this way, "They have conquered him [the devil] by the blood of the Lamb and by the word of their testimony, for they loved not their lives even unto death." Stand with God as if your life depends on it. The truth is, your life really does depend on it.

Right now, I encourage you to declare that you will respond to your life struggle by following God wholeheartedly and without turning back. You are either 100 percent in . . . or not. You are either going to follow God . . . or not. Otherwise, the only one you are fooling is you. Being lukewarm in your walk with the Lord serves no positive purpose, to state it mildly. In fact, Jesus commented on a church called Laodicea which was trying to be on both sides of the proverbial fence; "'I know your works: you are neither cold nor hot. Would that you were either cold or hot! So, because you are lukewarm, and neither hot nor cold, I will spit you out of my mouth'" (Revelation 3:15–16).

Put on the whole armor of God! Fight by God's rules from this day forward. Declare as Joshua did when considering his future, "But as for me and my house, we will serve the Lord" (Joshua 24:15). Initially, this will cause you great discomfort because you may be tempted to respond to your offender in the way he or she hurt you. But if you are faithful to take the high road—God's road—then you will be rewarded.

Paul's strategy to winning life's battles begins with Victory Action 1: Put on the Whole Armor of God. This action will equip you to stand firm against the evil one. Like Destroyer in our boxing story, he will punch away at you but will ultimately give up and run away. Note that once you put on the whole armor of God and declare that you will live and fight by Jesus' rules, you will be challenged. But it is at that exact moment that your life situation will be transformed from one of hopeless despair to one of victory.

I believe that the Old Testament version of putting on the whole armor of God is found in Psalm 91. The first verse states: "He who dwells in the shelter of the Most High will abide in the shadow of the Almighty." When you side fully with God then you are in His presence. In His presence there is joy, peace, purpose, and fulfillment.

Take a moment now and read aloud all of Psalm 91. As you read the rewards of being on God's side, be encouraged that this is indeed your best option and that you will be on the road to victory.

Once you determined in your heart to put on the whole armor of God, you can then address the next step in Paul's winning strategy, "Victory Action 2: Stand Firm"

FOR YOU TO CONSIDER

1. Why does responding to your battle by the rules of your old nature fall short of bringing you victory?

2. What does it mean to "live and fight by Jesus' rules"?

3. List three actions you will take that reveal you are fighting by "Jesus' rules."

4. List three of the benefits of putting on God's armor that resonated with you. State why they made an impression on you and what your response will be to each one.

5. Find someone who has found victory and allow that person to encourage you.

6. Write a prayer to the Lord in response to this chapter.

SCRIPTURE FOR YOU TO PRAY TODAY

"Father, if you are willing, remove this cup from me. Nevertheless, not my will, but yours, be done" (Luke 22:42).

What is the Lord saying to you right now?

VICTORY ACTION 2

STAND FIRM

DECLARE WHO YOU WILL SERVE

"Therefore take up the whole armor of God, that you may be able to withstand in the evil day, and having done all, to stand firm."

EPHESIANS 6:13

"No temptation has overtaken you that is not common to man. God is faithful, and he will not let you be tempted beyond your ability, but with the temptation he will also provide the way of escape, that you may be able to endure it."

1 CORINTHIANS 10:13

I remember vividly the day that the doctor told us that there was a high probability that our third child would not be healthy when born. I was too stunned to speak or even move! It was as if every fiber in my being came to a screeching halt. But within a few seconds, I felt the Lord put into my heart this thought, "We will love this baby with all our hearts no matter what his condition may be. This child is a gift from God and we will shower him with love." I thank the Lord that He gave me the wisdom that day to draw the proverbial line in the sand and declare my position. From that moment on, there was no reversal, retreat, or second-guessing. Praise the Lord, four months later, our son was born completely healthy.

Once you put on the whole armor of God you must now implement Paul's strategy to winning life's battle Victory Action 2: Stand Firm. You are going to fight by God's rules no matter what happens. Making such a declaration is vital to the rebuilding of your life because it will serve as an anchor in the midst of the storms of life. The ebb and flow of your existence will challenge your desire to act in a manner that honors God and will seek to knock you off course from where God wants you to be.

Like Joshua, you must declare "whom you will serve" and stick with your plan that says, "But as for me and my house, we will serve the LORD" (Joshua 24:15). It is in your best interest to state your position that you are either 100 percent following God or 100 percent not following God. Vacillating between the two only fools you, because truthfully, you are either following God or you are not. There is no middle ground. My prayer is that you will declare, this very moment, "As for me and my house, we will serve the LORD!" If you do, then you are on the road to recovery. If you do not, then your plan is like fool's gold and you will never recover fully.

Standing firm in the middle of a fight does not always come naturally to us. Chances are, when life knocked you down, you believed instinctively that you should either counter-attack or run away. As we discussed earlier, the fight or flight response is usually not the best response in your current circumstance.

Fighting the one who hurt you places you in a reactive position. If you fight, then you must question by whose rules are you fighting; God's rules or those of someone else. You know that if you follow the Lord that He will give you "a crown of beauty instead of ashes, the oil of joy instead of mourning, and a garment of praise instead of a spirit of despair" (Isaiah 61:3, NIV). What will result if you respond by the rules of anyone else? Probably, you will make matters even worse, you will cause further pain, and you will be forced to live with a lifetime of regret. Plus, fighting back at the one who hurt you lowers you to the level of your offender and you are equally as guilty at that point.

Fleeing the situation—either physically, emotionally, by not taking responsibility—also brings a negative outcome. You can avoid the situation for a time, but eventually you must encounter it. At that point, the encounter will hurt even more; like ripping open an old wound. If you know your Bible at all, then you know how God wants you to respond in the situation. If you avoid responding in a manner that honors God, you will be like Jonah who ran away, rather than fulfill God's will. Life became even worse for Jonah until he repented and obeyed God.

Adam and Eve serve as a classic example of how you do not want to respond when you are knocked to the canvas by temptation. You could say when God held them accountable for their behavior that they did both—fight and flight. They fought back by trying to defend their actions and then they ran away by hiding from God's presence and by refusing responsibility for their behavior.

Since hindsight is 20/20, we can examine the mistakes made by Eve when she was knocked down by the devil as recorded in Genesis 3. Her mistakes were (1) she dialogued with the devil, (2) she considered the devil as a credible source who could make a more valid point than God, (3) she allowed the devil to plant seeds of doubt toward God in her heart—"did God *actually* say" (Genesis 3:31, emphasis added), (4) she took her focus off her relationship with God and considered how pleasing the fruit looked to her, and (5) she blamed the devil instead of taking responsibility for her actions.

> It is vital to your emotional and spiritual health that you consider these voices through the filter of God's Word. If what you are hearing does not align itself to God's Word then those voices must be rejected!

Adam's misplayed this episode as well when he did the following: (1) he did not stand as the spiritual authority in the relationship and say that eating the fruit was wrong, (2) he allowed his guilt to override his sense of accountability before God as seen when he and Eve hid from God, and (3) he blamed Eve and God—"The woman whom you gave to be with me, she gave me fruit of the tree, and I ate" (Genesis 3:12).

No matter what life used to knock you down, you will be tempted to make the same mistakes as those made by Eve and Adam. There are voices in your head, voices from the media, and even voices from friends who are well-meaning telling you how to respond to your current life drama. It is vital to your emotional and spiritual health that you consider these voices through the filter of God's Word. If what you are hearing does not align itself to God's Word then those voices must be rejected!

I know how hard it is to "turn the other check" (see Matthew 5:39). I know how easy it is to blame the one who hurt you! Somehow, we seem to find solace in taking the stance of being a victim and reciting the outrageous wrongs of our offender. Even though you may indeed be the victim, such a response to being knocked down by life wastes your emotional energy and focuses on the incidents rather than on the solutions. The fact is you cannot change the one who hurt you. However, you can determine how you will respond!

It is shocking to me how readily Adam was to blame God for his behavior! I have been equally guilty of this at times in my life. But it makes as little sense as when we saw Champ, in my story of the boxer, get knocked to the canvas and turn to blame the referee. The devil wants you to blame God for your current predicament! If you do, you will alienate yourself from the Answer, the very One who is Truth and Love.

So you are now at the crossroads of how you will rebuild your life. If you respond like Eve and Adam then you will receive the same results. If you follow the apostle Paul's Victory Action 2: Stand Firm, then you will rebuild your life on a solid foundation and reap the benefits for the rest of your life.

Four times in our Ephesians 6 passage, we are told to "stand against the schemes of the devil" (verse 11), "withstand in the evil day" (verse 13), "stand firm" (verse 13), and "stand" (verse 14) The repetition of the word, "stand," reveals it is of the highest importance. The quality of your life will be proportional directly to your ability to stand firm by standing with God. Thankfully, we have an example from our Lord to see how we can stand firm in the face of a spiritual attack.

In Matthew 4:1–11, we read about the time Jesus went to the desert and fasted for forty days and forty nights. The Bible says, "he was hungry." It was at this point, when he was physically and emotionally weakened, that the devil entered the scene to tempt Him three times.

The temptations began with the devil demanding that Jesus prove His deity to him. "If you are the Son of God," the devil demanded. But who is the devil that he should demand anything from the Son of God? Jesus was not required to prove Himself to anyone but God the Father. So Jesus stood firm immediately by not engaging the devil in conversation about the devil's false authority.

The devil then went to the first temptation: "If you are the Son of God, command these stones to become loaves of bread." But instead of fighting the devil physically or with a war of words and instead of running away, Jesus responded to the evil one with the Truth of God's Word. "Jesus answered, 'It is written: "Man shall not live by bread alone, but by every word that comes from the mouth of God."'" The temptation before Jesus was to delve into the pleasures of the flesh but He stood firm by declaring the Truth of God's Word.

As you decide how you will respond to being knocked down by life, you must determine whether you will seek the quickest and easily way to rebuild your life or if you will declare that you will follow the right way. As we discussed earlier, when someone hurts you, you are tempted to hurt your offender more because you think it will restore your sense of justice and make you feel better in the short term. This is not the response that honors the Lord. Instead, as you follow God's Word by obeying Jesus' teaching in the Sermon on the Mount in Matthew 5–7, you will reap your greatest benefit in the long term.

The second temptation appealed to Jesus' pride. The devil wanted Jesus to show off His position as the Son of God. But Jesus stood firm by standing on the Word of God again as His authority.

Jesus received His sense of self-worth and His identity from God the Father and not from the fickle approvals of others.

As you consider how you will react to your current personal drama, you must ask yourself if your plan of action is rooted in seeking truth and righteousness or if you are actually just lashing out because your pride was hurt. Thoughts like, "Who does he think that I am?" and "She can't do that to me!" are probably rooted in pride, and thus, you are on shaky ground from the start when trying to defend yourself. Like Jesus, your sense of self-worth and your identity must come from being a child of God.

The third temptation was for Jesus to proclaim Himself to be all powerful and rule all the kingdoms of the world. The price for having it all was that He would owe his soul to the devil. This was ludicrous from the very mention because, while the devil has his authority for a time, his demise is well documented in the Bible. So he is not worthy to be worshipped at any time. Jesus stood firm **True power comes from obeying God's Word, especially in the most difficult moments of life, and then allowing the Lord to take care of the consequences.** by remaining consistent in His response. He acted righteously by quoting the Truth and by relying on God the Father.

You have been knocked to the canvas of life. You know you must determine in your heart whose path you will follow. Fighting by the devil's rules will bring some sense of accomplishment but that is fleeting. Sure, you might get revenge and you might even fool yourself into thinking that you can elevate your life by degrading your offender. But such power is valued only by the weak-minded and the morally spineless. Proverbs 14:12 states it this way, "There is a way that seems right to a man, but its end is the way to death." True power comes from obeying God's Word, especially in the most difficult moments of life, and then allowing the Lord to take care of the consequences.

I hope that you are ready to make the declaration that you will stand firm. This is a definitive "draw the line in the sand" moment where you declare, like Joshua, "As for me and my house, we will serve the LORD" (Joshua 24:15). And you must live this declaration each day.

If you are still in shock from being knocked down by life, then living this declaration can be challenging. Start where you are emotionally and build to where you want to be. Before your feet hit the floor in the morning, pray and ask Jesus to stand with you and to give you the strength to stand firm throughout the day. Living this declaration may mean that you try to stand firm for one hour. The Lord will give you strength. After doing this for some time, you will soon grow to ask the Lord to give you strength to stand firm for the morning. He will do so because He stands with you. After a time, you will stand firm for a whole day, and then an entire week. The point is if you are faithful to stand firm for as long as you can, then the Lord will help you to build on that commitment and lead you in rebuilding your life.

> **The point is if you are faithful to stand firm for as long as you can, then the Lord will help you to build on that commitment and lead you in rebuilding your life.**

This process reminds me of the passage in Philippians 4 where Paul writes, "Not that I am speaking of being in need, for I have learned in whatever situation I am to be content" (Philippians 4:11, NIV). Living your declaration to stand firm will teach you to be content regardless of the circumstances. Initially, standing firm will not seem to make much difference in your life. But as you stand consistently, you will begin to see tangible differences in your life such as regaining your emotional and physical strength, as well as having your joy for life return.

The Philippians passage continues, "I know what it is to be in need, and I know what it is to have plenty. I have learned the secret of being content in any and every situation, whether well fed or hungry, whether living in plenty or in what. I can do all this through him who gives me strength" (Philippians 4:12–13, NIV). Another translation reads, "I can do all things through Christ who strengthens me" (NKJV). If you stand with the Lord, you will learn to be content no matter what the circumstance. The Lord will give you strength!

The remainder of our key passage—Ephesians 6:10–20—will give us direction as to how we can stand firm with the Lord and rebuild our lives. We put on the whole armor of God and standing firm in truth, righteousness, peace, faith, salvation, and the Word of God, as well as, praying in the Spirit and caring for others. The more we are faithful to stand firm each day, the more we will see the tide of doubt, anger, and feeling like a victim subside and the growing tidal wave of hope, restoration, and even joy will one day define our daily walk.

FOR YOU TO CONSIDER

1. Why are fighting and fleeing not appropriate responses?

2. What does Jesus' response when He was tempted by the devil teach you about standing firm?

3. Remind yourself that learning to stand firm is a process. Read again Philippians 4:12–13 and then compose a prayer to ask the Lord for help in this endeavor.

SCRIPTURE FOR YOU TO PRAY TODAY

"But as for me and my house, we will serve the LORD" (Joshua 24:15).

What is the Lord saying to you right now?

VICTORY ACTION 3

LIVE IN TRUTH

FOCUS ON THE ONE WHO IS TRUTH

"Stand therefore, having fastened on the belt of truth."

EPHESIANS 6:14A

"If you hold to my teaching, you are really my disciples. Then you will know the truth, and the truth will set you free."

JOHN 8:32, NIV

O n the night that Jesus was betrayed, tortured, and suffered a horrific death on the cross, He endured mock trials before religious leaders and political figures. Jesus stood before Pilate, who represented Rome, because the Jewish leaders did not have the authority to enforce the death penalty. The Jewish leaders had to convince Pilate that Jesus was a criminal whose crimes were against Rome and were worthy of execution.

It was during Jesus' interview with Pilate that He said, "You say that I am a king. For this purpose I was born and for this purpose I have come into the world—to bear witness to the truth. Everyone who is of the truth listens to my voice" (John 18:37). Pilate then asked, "What is truth?" (John 18:38). What a ridiculous question!

Jesus is the very definition of Truth! He is Truth! Even though He is Creator standing before His creation, He stood willingly as one accused falsely of crimes against God and against Rome, and before self-righteous and self-proclaimed authorities. How outrageous! Then Pilate, in the presence of "the way, the truth, and the life" (John 14:6) had the gall to ask, "What is truth?" Jesus was standing right in front of him. He was so close that Pilate could literally touch the One who is fully God and fully man, and yet he was blinded by his sin. Unbelievable!

The Jewish officials who brought Jesus before Pilate had their version of the truth: they wanted to protect their power and authority. The crowd had their version of the truth: some were influenced by the Jewish officials while others wanted Jesus to be the political leader who would defeat the Romans. Pilate had his version of the Truth: he saw himself being the true authority in this drama. Even many of those who genuinely followed Jesus saw truth as being that which would usher in a new day for the nation of Israel. Only Jesus understood the Truth.

Since you were knocked to the canvas of life, you have been struggling to make sense of it all! No doubt, your mind is reeling and you asking, "What is going on?" "How can this be happening?" "How could he (or she) do this to me?" "What's going to happen next?" All these heart-felt and important questions are forms of the same question that Pilate asked; "What is truth?"

Voices around you are flooding your mind and heart and presenting their version of truth. You have people at work offering their advice as to how you should respond to your personal dilemma. You have voices from the media presenting their philosophy of overcoming the odds and winning. Even your friends with the best intentions give you their advice, but their thoughts are tainted by their experiences and motivations. So what is truth? Whose truth should you follow?

The voice that is most difficult to understand is often the voice of your offender. Someone you trusted, believed in, or considered a friend on some level, now is telling you a new reality that makes no sense to you. The voice sounds familiar but the message is vastly different.

It reminds me of a story of a man who worked for a company for seven years. One day he received an e-mail from his boss that, without prior warning or discussion, he was to be replaced in his current role. He was to be given a lesser role in another location, all due to comments made to the boss by those subordinate to the man. Seven years of working, and in a moment's notice, he was removed from his place of authority and relocated. The man was crushed! He was being told that his work was subpar, that he had mishandled finances, and that his relationships with his subordinates were inappropriate and unprofessional. Yet he knew in his heart that none of this was true! If he had opportunity to discuss this matter with his boss, he would go issue by issue and defend his actions. The man became so discouraged that he questioned if he should continue with the company. His boss who was previously encouraging and supportive, turned into someone spouting a "truth" that did not align with the man's actions or motivations. Yet the man questioned himself and wondered if this was indeed the voice of truth.

I know that you are hurting right now. I know that your initial response to being hit is to see it as an unwarranted attack on you, the innocent victim. This might be the complete truth! And yet, it is in your best interest to see if there is any truth to what your offender is saying. Proverbs 15:31 puts it this way, "The ear that listens to life-giving reproof will dwell among the wise." So the first way that you can live Victory Action 3: Live in Truth is to consider if there is any truth to what your offender is saying.

Let's say that you are in a tail-spin because, like the man in my story, your boss just fired you. How could he do that? How are you going to pay the bills? How are you going to find another job in this economy? These are all valid questions! But did you stop to consider that your boss may have legitimate reasons for asking you to empty your desk? If you do not stop and address the truth of why you were fired then you are doomed to continue that behavior in your next job and you will probably be fired again! Truthfully, maybe you needed to be fired! After your hurt and anger subsides and stabilizes, take time to honestly assess your actions and behaviors. Learn from your mistakes! Look for ways to honor Christ in your workplace. I heard it put this way: dealing with the truth may cause you to take two steps backward in the short term, but eventually, it will sling-shot you to a better life. The truth hurts, but the truth heals, too!

A second way for you to live Victory Action 3: Live in Truth is to know the truth about our spiritual enemy, the devil. The evil one wants us to focus on his lies and to consider them as if they are valid. He is a master manipulator who wants us to be tossed on the waves of chaos and confusion. The antidote to his tactics is to find truth and to live in truth. Truth is the anchor that keeps us steady when we find ourselves in the storms of life. Truth is the lighthouse that brings us hope and direction for rescue in the middle of the upheaval of life's storms.

There is so much that I could share with you about our spiritual enemy, but I will mention just two truths about him. The first truth is that all that is "bad" originates from the devil. The evil one has power in this world for a time and uses it to kill and destroy everything and everyone created and loved by God. The devil knows the Truth of God's Word. Yet he still believe his own lies; lies that say one day he will defeat God. Yet he knows that he cannot hurt God. So he goes after the ones who God loves the most, God's children, in an effort to destroy them and crush God's heart. In Romans 5:12–21, Paul wrote that sin entered the world through one man, Adam, and brought death. So the origin of sin and death is the devil. But note also that this same passage brings hope. It states that just as sin entered the world through one man, Adam, God's grace entered the world through one man, Jesus Christ.

You may be facing a life-threatening illness, a loss of job, the betrayal of a spouse, or a natural disaster. While you may know the individual who is at fault, the one who originated all sin, evil, and death is the devil. As we discussed earlier, the object of your anger and wrath should not be God, but ultimately the devil. Get mad at the one who originated sin and death!

The truth is that God is good and only that which is good comes from Him. The Bible says it this way,

> *Let no one say when he is tempted, "I am being tempted by God," for God cannot be tempted with evil, and he himself tempts no one. But each person is tempted when he is lured and enticed by his own desire. Then desire when it has conceived gives birth to sin, and sin when it is fully grown brings forth death. Do not be deceived, my beloved brothers. Every good gift and every perfect gift is from above, coming down from the Father of lights, with whom there is no variation or shadow due to change. Of his own will he brought us forth by the word of truth, that we should be a kind of firstfruits of his creatures (James 1:13–18).*

The second truth about our spiritual enemy is that the devil's main tactic is to cause you to doubt. We mentioned this earlier but it is important to repeat it. When bad things happen to good people, the devil tries to whisper in your ear that God is not in control. He wants you to question, "God, why did you not save me?" or "God, do you not care about me?" Once again, I remind you of Genesis 3. In the Garden of Eden, when the serpent asked Eve, "Did God actually say, 'You shall not eat of any tree in the garden?'" The devil wants you to think that he has the authority and the right to question God.

After he gets you to doubt God, he wants you to doubt yourself. He will tell you that you are no good, you have no value, you are alone, and no one cares. He lies about God not being in control and he lies about your self-worth. He wants you to be inundated by the voices of this world that present their wisdom and experience as if it were truth. Thankfully, the Bible is filled to overflowing with truths that overcome the doubts of the devil.

The third way that you can fulfill Victory Action 3: Live in Truth is to replace the outside voices that you hear with the Truth of in God's Word. Every single day, you must declare Truth to yourself and live in the light of this Truth, even when you do not feel like it.

Every single day, you must tell yourself that God is in control. Right now, the focus of your mind and heart is on your pain. In fact, it is so bad that you wonder if you will ever be able to breathe without making a concerted effort. Even though you cannot see the finish line to this life struggle and even though you feel that you are without any hope, you must remember that God is in control. This season of life will pass, you will survive, and you will emerge in victory because you allow God to control and rebuild your life.

We live in a world where it rains on the just and the unjust. Bad things happen to good people and to bad people. This is the result of our living in a world corrupted by sin. In spite of this, God is still in control. The story of Joseph makes the point that while Joseph's brothers had evil intentions and sold him into slavery, God was still in control. Joseph was placed strategically by God in Pharaoh's presence to bring God glory. Once all was revealed, Joseph told his brothers, "You intended to harm me, but God intended it for good to accomplish what is now being done, the saving of many lives" (Genesis 50:20, NIV).

There are times when we want Jesus to return immediately and balance the scales of justice. But even with all the wars and rumors of wars and worldwide tragedies, God is still in control. In 2 Peter 3:9 we read, "The Lord is not to fulfill his promise, as some count slowness, but is patient toward you, not wishing that any should perish, but that all should reach repentance."

There is one more important verse that I will share on this point: Romans 8:28. "And we know that for those who love God all things work together for good, for those who are called according to his purpose." When you encounter life's battles, stand firm on the truth that God is in control and will work all things for His glory.

> **When you accepted Jesus Christ as your Savior and Lord, you became a child of God and an heir to the King. You matter to God. He loves you unconditionally.**

Every single day, you must tell yourself that you are God's child. You do not have to doubt His love for you or doubt to whom you belong. When you accepted Jesus Christ as your Savior and Lord, you became a child of God and an heir to the King. You matter to God. He loves you unconditionally. The natural reaction to being knocked to the canvas of life is to doubt your self-worth and wonder if your life will ever amount to anything noteworthy. You may even feel that you are a failure due to a loss of a relationship, a loss of a job, or the death of a loved one. While these aspects of life are important, they do not define who you are.

The truth is that you are a child of God and that you belong to Him. God did not define you—or love you—because of your job, your role in life, or for what you can do for Him. He loves you unconditionally. You matter to God! You have worth and value because God loves you! This is truth Stand firm and live in Truth. Romans 8:31 affirms this: "If God is for us, who can be against us?" and a few verses later in verse 37, "No, in all these things we are more than conquerors through him who loved us."

> You matter to God! You have worth and value because God loves you! This is truth.

Every single day, you must tell yourself that God keeps His promises. The Bible is God's letter to you that reveals His character and His love for you. It teaches us that God loved you so much that He sent Jesus Christ to die for your sins. Jesus loves you so much that He gave His life willingly and rose again on the third day, conquering sin and death. You can live in the Truth that Jesus is alive and walks with you throughout life's journey! God does not promise you will never face a battle in life. However, He did promise that He will never leave you or forsake you and that He will fight life's battles for you!

Every single day, you must tell yourself that Jesus is Truth and so you will follow Him and His ways. As we discussed earlier, many voices are screaming at you to fight back or to run away or to see revenge. Instead, determine steadfastly that you will stand firm, living by God's rules. Every day, you must declare that you will follow Jesus. Every day, stand firm in the truth that the way out of this nightmare is to follow Christ. Stand firm in the truth that Jesus said, "I am the way, and the truth, and the life. No one comes to the Father except through me" (John 14:6). He taught also, "If you abide in my word, you are truly my disciples, and you will know the truth, and the truth will set you free" (John 8:31–32).

The fourth way that you can fulfill Victory Action 3: Live in Truth is to determine to respond to life's challenges in a manner that honors Christ. Your goal is to follow closely the Truth of Jesus Christ so that you will honor Him and will live without regret. Believing the lies of the enemy or the one who hurt you does not honor Christ because it is not truth. Seeking to hurt, disparage, or engage in any form of retaliation toward your offender may bring seeming satisfaction in the short term. However, once the heat of passion cools, you will find yourself not only dealing with your pain, but now wallowing in the guilt and shame of your reaction: regret.

You can find victory in the midst of the ferocious storms of life by determining to respond in ways that honor Christ. For example, when your spouse has an affair and abandons you and your children, speak words of honor only about that spouse to your children or do not speak at all. While you do not lie about the spouse either in effort to speak good, you must realize that your words of anger and hurt will sow seeds of bitterness in your home. Otherwise, you will rue the day of your unwise words and you will reap a harvest of anger in your children. You will live to regret reacting to sin with more sin.

If you choose to speak that which brings honor or not speak at all, then you will reap a harvest of righteousness. I know that, in the short term, every fiber in your being wants to spout off and declare the "truth" of your situation and the reason for your unending pain. But if you honor God by living by the Truth of His Word, He will honor you. In the long term, and this is where you live the rest of your life, you will find refuge and eventually relief from the storms of life. Live without regret by honoring Christ in every thought, every conversation, every day, and in every way, and you will live in victory.

The fifth way that you can fulfill Victory Action 3: Live in Truth is to surround yourself with people who know Truth. Find people who will encourage you and challenge you to live in Truth and allow them to speak Truth into your life. Rid yourself immediately of friendships and relationships with people who do not practice the Truth of God's Word and who encourage you to consider reactions that do not honor Christ.

Live without regret by honoring Christ in every thought, every conversation, every day, and in every way, and you will live in victory.

When I was going through my darkest hour, the Lord blessed me with a man of God who counseled me. Instead of focusing on my offender, he directed my attention to me—my thoughts, my reactions, and my goals to live in victory. It was during each conversation that he would take me back to the Bible. God's Word became my bread of life that fed me Truth each day. Instead of continually hitting the rewind button of my mind to consider how life had beat me down or wasting emotional energy plotting revenge, he led me focus on the Truth of God's Word. In doing so, I was rebuilding my life even when I was emotionally and physically weak.

I encourage you strongly to take this course of action. Sitting with your friends and telling your tale of woe will bring relief, but it will be fleeting. You are dealing with the symptoms of the problem and not the core issues. Your friends will voice their opinions freely, some of them with impassioned pleas, but if they do not speak Truth, then your conversations are nothing but hot air and amount to nothing. It will not take long to discover that if your pain becomes the center of your conversations with them, then they will distance themselves from you.

Surround yourself with friends who live and breathe and speak Truth. These are true friends. They will speak the truth to you. They will stand with you during the trial. If you ask the Lord to bring you such friends, you will be surprised at who He will choose. You might discover that He will bring people into your life so you can form new friendships; friendships that will last a lifetime.

"What is truth?" This is a question that each of us will encounter many times in our lives. Jesus Christ is the Truth. Align your heart, mind, soul, and strength to Him. When you do, you are on the path to healing, to rebuilding, and to victory.

FOR YOU TO CONSIDER

1. What truth, if any, is there to what your offender is saying to you? What actions must you take in response?

2. Who is the source of your dilemma? Who is truly on your side to protect and defend you?

3. Write your feelings and thoughts that you have presently about yourself and your personal drama in your journal. How does this compare to how Jesus feels about you as revealed in the Bible? Remember, God is not the author of lies, chaos, or anxiety, so any such thoughts are not from Him.

4. List three promises from God's Word that apply to you. State aloud each promise and declare that you will live by Truth. Set a time in your daily calendar when you will read these promises and when you will make this declaration.

5. Identify three friends with whom you should spend time and allow them to speak Truth into your life. List any friends whom you should avoid because their words or actions are not edifying.

SCRIPTURE FOR YOU TO PRAY TODAY

"If you abide in my word, you are truly my disciples, and you will know the truth, and the truth will set you free" (John 8:31–32).

What is the Lord saying to you right now?

VICTORY ACTION 4

LIVE IN RIGHTEOUSNESS
LIVE WITH INTENTIONALITY

*"Stand therefore, . . . having put on the
breastplate of righteousness."*

EPHESIANS 6:14B

*"For God gave us a spirit not of fear but of power
and love and self-control."*

2 TIMOTHY 1:7

They had what seemed to be the storybook marriage. He was
the captain of the football team and she was the head of
the cheerleading squad. After graduation, they married,
had two children, a dog, a beautiful home, and a scenic waterfront
vacation home. They had the fairy-tale life: looks, wealth, kids, and
respect from others at church and at work. It was perfect—at least,
that's what it looked like on the surface. In reality, he worked late

hours, she became bored with their life, they were in financial debt, and the kids focused on their friends and video games instead of family communication. They became so busy with life that they neglected their personal devotional time in God's Word and their church attendance decreased. You've heard the story!

The wife decided that her needs are not being met, that she needed someone to flaunt money and praise on her, so she committed adultery with a married man. Their secret trysts were soon discovered by her best friend. The husband learned of the affair, drove to the hotel where his wife was meeting the other man and became enraged. He was ready to break down the hotel room door, with a baseball bat in hand, and beat the other man. Fortunately, his cell phone rang and a close friend talked him out of making a huge mistake.

The husband decided to "show her a thing or two," found a much younger woman than his wife and began an affair of his own. He figured that he would teach his wife a lesson.

You've heard this story of destruction before and so I will spare you more details! The "perfect" marriage ended in divorce. The husband started living with a woman with whom he was not married. The wife eventually married numerous times. The children were standing on the sidelines of their parents' drama. Feeling neglected and unloved, they were doomed to repeat this cycle of destruction.

Paul's strategy to winning life's battles so far was to put on the whole armor of God, to stand firm, to live in truth and now we consider Victory Action 4: Live in Righteousness. There are two points you need to know about righteousness. First, righteousness is positional. When you repent of your sins and accept Jesus Christ as your Savior and Lord, you are then forgiven, cleansed, and made into a new creation. Jesus Christ makes you righteous. This new identity, as His disciple, gains you entrance into the presence of God as a son or daughter relating to the Heavenly Father.

Second, righteousness is your choice. While you are made righteous when you are saved, you must choose to live a righteous life until you are in heaven and living righteously for eternity. Life brings victories and defeats—mountaintop experiences of ecstatic joy and deflating episodes that feel completely overwhelmed.

You have been knocked to the canvas of life. You are in pain emotionally, spiritually, and perhaps even physically. You wonder if this nightmare will ever end! What should you do now? Well, now is the time to take the next step to rebuilding: Begin living with intentionality. You must determine in your heart and mind that you will live righteously.

> Now is the time to take the next step to rebuilding: Begin living with intentionality. You must determine in your heart and mind that you will live righteously.

It is not a mistake that Paul instructed you to put on the "breastplate of righteousness." The breastplate was a form of body armor that covered the soldier's entire upper body and protected his heart and other vital organs. Life's knockdowns can be issues that directly involve matters of the heart, such as death or divorce; or they may be issues that cause ripples that impact loved ones, such as financial difficulties or failing health. The battle you face now is focusing your energies and actions on what your mind tells you is the right reaction, instead of responding out of the brokenness of your heart. In other words, standing firm in righteousness means that you choose to do what is right, to live righteously, instead of being driven by your feelings and emotions. This is what is referred to in 2 Timothy 1:7 as "self-control" or in other translations as "self-discipline."

We discussed this earlier, but I want to emphasize that you must determine, especially right now, that you are going to rebuild your life by living righteously. That means that you will live by God's rules. There are three actions that you must do.

First, in order to live righteously, you must believe that God is in control of your life, your situation, and your future. Romans 8:28 reads, "And we know that for those who love God all things work together for good, for those who are called according to his purpose."

In fact, pause right now and personalize Romans 8:28 as your prayer: "Dear God, I thank you that in all things, You work for my good, because I love You and have been called for Your purpose." Trust me in this: even though you cannot fathom the future, God has His plans ready for you and He will journey with you to fulfill His destiny for you!

You may be wondering, "What possible good can result from my tragedy?" While I cannot answer this question specifically, I do know that when you turn to God in the midst of your personal drama, you will discover a depth of relationship with Him that you never knew. God hears the cry of your heart and responds with His presence in your heart and mind as you read the Word, as you worship, and as you pour out your heart to Him in prayer.

When you turn to God, your recovery and the re-creation of your life will be built on the most solid of all foundations: Jesus Christ. The couple in the story at the beginning of this chapter did not live by God's rules, but instead, were ruled by the emotions resulting from wounded hearts. They built their new lives on the foundation of selfishness, pain, revenge, and mistrust. They were doomed to failure the moment they made the decision to live by the rules of the world. However, living in the presence of God and following His rules will get you out of the darkness of this season and into the light of a new day.

If you have children, you will discover that they are watching and learning how you respond to getting knocked down and how God helps you recover. If you live by God's rules, then a result of the tragedy would be that you are equipping your children to handle life properly when they have their own experiences. This is how the cycle of destruction mentioned in our story is broken. You can replace it with the cycle of life!

Second, in order to live righteously, you must determine to let God fight your battle for you and allow Him to balance the scales of justice. Romans 12:19 states, "Beloved, never avenge yourselves, but leave it to the wrath of God, for it is written, 'Vengeance is mine, I will repay, says the Lord.'" If you seek revenge, you will never escape the trap of offense: he hurt you, you hurt him back, so he hurts you, and that causes you to hurt him. The trap of offense can cause feuds to fester for decades, hurt innocent lives, and cause people to carry burdens that they should not carry. In fact, what happens is people are driven by intense hatred and forget the reason for the original offense!

If you allow God to avenge you, then you know that the scales of justice will be balanced. If you place yourself in the role of God, then what punishment is appropriate for the hurt and suffering imposed on you? Are you willing to walk with your offender through the process of sentencing, punishment, and rebuilding? I do not think so. Besides, that is not your role; it belongs to God!

If you allow God to avenge you, then you are freed to focus on you! You can wash your hands of the offender and the offense, and begin to rebuild and re-create your life. Leave your offender in God's hands. Walk away! Only God can change the heart of your offender. Focus on your heart, on your relationship with the Lord, and the future that He has for you.

Third, in order to live righteously, you must live rightly! Here is the formula that I was taught about how to live righteously: do the right action, in the right way, for the right reason, and for the right outcome. As I share this with you, please remember that you must choose to live righteously. There will be days when your old nature rises up and screams at you to get revenge, to hurt your offender as you were hurt, or to look out for yourself! Instead, ask the Lord to give you strength each day to put on the "spirit of . . . self-control" as Paul wrote to Timothy. Living righteously is your choice!

> **Here is the formula that I was taught about how to live righteously: do the right action, in the right way, for the right reason, and for the right outcome.**

TO LIVE RIGHTEOUSLY MEANS YOU WILL DO THE RIGHT ACTION . . .

This means that you will respond to life's trials in the ways taught you in the Bible. Using an old cliché, you will take the high road every day and in every way. Paul's winning strategy up to this point applies here! You must put on the whole armor of God, stand firm, and live in Truth each day, and in doing so, you are doing the right action, the right thing. Living by God's rules may seem difficult, at times, and it may not bring the immediate result that you desire. However, it will bring a lifetime of reward in the long term. Paul stated it this way, "Do not be deceived: God is not mocked, for whatever one sows, that will he also reap. For the one who sows to his own flesh will from the flesh reap corruption, but the one who sows to the Spirit will from the Spirit reap eternal life. And let us not grow weary of doing good, for in due season we will reap, if we do not give up" (Galatians 6:7–9).

IN THE RIGHT WAY . . .

Determine that as you stand firm against the attacks that you will do so in the strength of the Lord. In my personal drama, when I was cast away, I told my three sons that we were going to draw the proverbial line in the sand and declare that we will live for the Lord. We attended church every time services were held; Sunday morning, Sunday night, Wednesday night pre-service prayer, Wednesday night prayer service, and even home groups. The right way to respond to a single-parent home with three boys was to live for the Lord without turning back, without regret, and without any doubts.

As the head of my home, the right way meant that I set the spiritual standard. I would only speak words of blessing about anyone who offended me, or I would say nothing at all. I encouraged my sons to love everyone in the family and to pray that they will hear from Jesus. If I allowed words of anger, bitterness, or depression in my home, then I was to blame. I could not change what happened in the past, but with the Lord's help and strength, I could determine what happens in the present and lay a solid foundation for the future.

The right way meant that I was trusting in the Lord to provide for all our needs; food, shelter, schools, a job, finances, and positive communication and love in our home. The right way meant that each day I prayed that the Lord would equip me to be the best dad, son, and servant that I could be. I prayed for my sons daily and I prayed that the Lord would fill our home with "love, joy, peace,

VICTORY ACTION 4: LIVE IN RIGHTEOUSNESS

patience, kindness, goodness, faithfulness, gentleness, and self-control" (Galatians 5:22–23).

Living the right way means that we do our best each day to apply the Truths of God's Word in our lives and homes. Honestly, some days are better than others! There were times when I was tired, angry, or not wanting to express myself in the right way. Fortunately, when I did make a mistake, I was smart enough to repent before the Lord, to admit this to the boys, and to ask for their forgiveness. Then, I made sure my inappropriate response was not repeated.

FOR THE RIGHT REASON . . .

Why should you do the right action and in the right way? Well, I can think of two reasons immediately. First, because you want to bring God glory. Right now, you are hurting. As you read this you might be thinking, "I know that I should want to bring God glory, but all I want is the pain to go away and for things to be the way it was before." I understand that thought completely! However, you are a believer, and if you could throw off the pain and suffering, you would find that you really do want to honor God in everything that you say and do. You are learning how to deal with suffering, and this allows you to capture a glimpse of how Jesus suffered. No one wants to suffer and no healthy person looks to suffer. However, life does

> **You are learning how to deal with suffering, and this allows you to capture a glimpse of how Jesus suffered. . . . You will understand better what Christ endured and you will greatly appreciate the victory when the Lord provides.**

knock you down and suffering, on some level, is inevitable. When you are suffering, you benefit greatly if you respond rightly for the reason of bringing God glory. You will understand better what Christ endured and you will greatly appreciate the victory when the Lord provides. Peter stated it this way, "But rejoice insofar as you share in Christ's sufferings, that you may be rejoice and be glad when his glory is revealed" (1 Peter 4:13).

Second, the right reason for living righteously is that you love God more than life itself. The genuine test of true love is not measuring one's heartbeat when you are enamored with another. The genuine test of love occurs when life falls apart, when the feelings are threatened by ambivalence, and when communication stops flowing.

In the Book of Job, Satan is before God and makes the claim that the only reason that Job loved Him was he was blessed abundantly by God. "Have you not put a hedge around him and his house and all that he has? You have blessed the work of his hands, and his possessions have increased in the land. But stretch out your hand and touch all that he has, and he will curse you to your face" (Job 1:9–11). But Job loved God more than life itself. Job had feelings. He was wounded in incredible ways and to the precipice of death, but "in all this, Job did not sin with his lips" (Job 2:10).

You are rebuilding your life. You must determine in your heart to live righteously because you love the Lord more than life itself. You are not a Christian only when you see blessing, and honor, and miracles. You can stand firm, even when your life seems to be in chaos, because you know the Lord will make good from what was meant for evil. One of my favorite verses is Joshua 1:9, "Have I not commanded you? Be strong and courageous. Do not be afraid; do not be discouraged, for the LORD you God will be with you wherever you go" (NIV).

FOR THE RIGHT OUTCOME

What is your desired outcome from your current trial? Whether you can return your life to the way it was, or whether you must start over completely, I believe that your desired outcomes are healing and rebuilding. If you participated in sports in some point in your life, you will remember that true athletes play to win! I know that some play for personal reasons like fame and fortune, but genuine ball players play to win; fame and fortune follow winners! Whatever your desired outcomes are and if they bring glory to God, keep them in mind like a finish line before a runner. Then, live righteously

> **Whatever your desired outcomes are and if they bring glory to God, keep them in mind like a finish line before a runner. Then, live righteously so that you can win the race.**

so that you can win the race. Paul did that and wrote, "I have fought the good fight, I have finished the race, I have kept the faith. Henceforth there is laid up for me the crown of righteousness, which the Lord, the righteous Judge, will award to me on that day, and not only to me but also to all who have loved his appearing" (2 Timothy 4:7–9). May this be your outcome, too!

King David wrote Psalm 37:1–9 to teach us in specific terms how we can live a righteous life:

> *1 Fret not yourself because of evildoers;*
> *be not envious of wrongdoers!*
> *2 For they will soon fade like the grass*
> *and wither like the green herb.*
> *3 Trust in the LORD, and do good;*
> *dwell in the land and befriend faithfulness.*

4 Delight yourself in the LORD,
  and he will give you the desires of your heart.
5 Commit your way to the LORD;
  trust in him, and he will act.
6 He will bring forth your righteousness like a light,
  and your justice as the noonday.
7 Be still before the LORD and wait patiently for him;
  fret not yourself over the one who prospers in his way,
  over the man who carries out evil devices!
8 Refrain from anger, and forsake wrath!
  Fret not yourself; it tends only to evil.
9 For the evildoer shall be cut off,
  but those who wait for the LORD shall inherit the land.

Let's consider what David wrote.

First, the Psalm tells us, "Fret not." This means that we are not to worry, to be anxious, or to be envious of those who do evil.

Second, we are told to "trust in the LORD, and do good." You must make the decision to trust in the Lord completely and to act like Jesus at all times.

Third, you must "delight yourself in the LORD." This means that you will remember the victories God gave you in your past. You will praise Him for who He is and for what He is doing now. You will celebrate in advance for the victory that He will bring you.

Fourth, you must "commit your way to the LORD." You must determine that you will follow Jesus completely and that you will not turn back. You will not compromise your faith and you will do what God's Word, the Bible, tells you to do.

Fifth, you must "be still before the LORD and wait patiently for him." God is fighting for you. He will balance the scales of justice. He works according to His timing for He knows everything. Anxiety and worry do not come from the Lord. You can reject those feelings and instead have peace that God will bring victory into your life.

Finally, we are told to "refrain from anger, and forsake wrath." Getting angry makes your problems worse! Instead, walk away from your anger and allow God to move on your behalf.

In effort to live righteously, you must not fret and instead, you should trust, take delight, commit your way, be still, and refrain from anger and turn from wrath. You must seek to do this every day, in every situation, and with everyone. Ask and the Lord will give you strength to do so. He will give you the wisdom to know when to be silent, when to speak blessings, and what to do.

> **Living by God's rules is the only way that will bring order from your chaos and bring you an ultimate outcome that will bless you and your family for generations.**

The results will be that the offense committed against you "will soon fade like the grass and wither." However, for you, "He will bring forth your righteousness as the light, and your justice like the noonday (Psalm 37:6). The Psalm ends with this promise, "The salvation of the righteous is from the LORD; he is their stronghold in time of trouble. The LORD helps them and delivers them; he delivers them from the wicked and saves them, because they take refuge in him" (Psalm 37:39–40).

As has been stated already, the only person that you can change in your personal drama is you. You must make the choice whether you stand firm by living in righteousness or if you will allow the storms of live to toss you around without hope of rescue. I promise you that if you draw the proverbial line in the sand, like Joshua when he declared, "As for me and my house, we will serve the LORD" (Joshua 24:15), then you will be on the road to victory. Living by God's rules is the only way that will bring order from your chaos and bring you an ultimate outcome that will bless you and your family for generations. May the Lord give you the strength and grace to live with intentionality.

FOR YOU TO CONSIDER

1. What must you do to replace "the cycle of destruction" with "the cycle of life"?

2. What emotions, thoughts, and behaviors must you change to allow God to fight your battles for you?

3. What is the "right action" in your personal story?

4. What is the "right way" in your drama?

5. What is "for the right reason" in your current situation?

6. What is "the right outcome" that you should be seeking?

7. Pray Psalm 37:1–9 as a personal prayer.

SCRIPTURE FOR YOU TO PRAY TODAY

"Do not be deceived: God is not mocked, for whatever one sows, that will he also reap. For the one who sows to his own flesh will from the flesh reap corruption, but the one who sows to the Spirit will from the Spirit reap eternal life. And let us not grow weary of doing good, for in due season we will reap, if we do not give up" (Galatians 6:7–9).

What is the Lord saying to you right now?

VICTORY ACTION 5

LIVE IN THE GOSPEL OF PEACE

BE CONFIDENT IN THE ONE TO WHOM YOU BELONG

"[Stand therefore, . . .] as shoes for your feet, having put on the readiness given by the gospel of peace."

EPHESIANS 6:15

"Now may the Lord of peace himself give you peace at all times and in every way. The Lord be with all of you."

2 THESSALONIANS 3:16

Recently, a family was knocked to the canvas of life by the news that the wife had cancer. The doctors would do their best, but there was no guarantee whatsoever that their efforts would succeed. The news was shocking, stunning, and paralyzing.

Immediately a flood of questions poured into their hearts as they tried to consider the implications of this news on them and their grown children. This couple had served the Lord all of their lives! They had given their lives in ministry and shared God's love willingly and joyfully to everyone they encountered. Of all people to hear the dreaded word, cancer, you have to wonder, "why them?" Truly, bad things happen to good people. Instead of allowing the debilitating news to determine their outlook on life, they turned to Jesus and discovered "the peace of God, which surpasses all understanding" (Philippians 4:7).

I remember watching an American football game on TV one Sunday afternoon and seeing a wide receiver get hit by the defensive back so hard that the announcer thought he was knocked out. From the defensive player's point of view, it was an amazing bone-jarring hit. The wide receiver probably had a different view as the play looked career threatening. The wide receiver did get to his feet. His legs were wobbly and he looked like he was clueless as to where he was at that moment. After two steps, he lost his balance and crashed back to the turf. He was out . . . and out cold.

Immediately after receiving the news of your personal tragedy, you found yourself staggering, trying to gain understanding in the midst of chaos, and seeking desperately to regain control of your life. But nothing seems to make sense anymore! Instead of enjoying a life put together strategically to your liking, suddenly the entirety of your existence is in jeopardy. And the myriad of subsequent questions overwhelms you.

Most of the questions you encounter are reduced to one word: Why? Why did I get fired from my job? Why did my spouse leave me? Why do I stand face to face with a deadly disease? Why me? It just does not make sense!

It is in this season of life that we are robbed of joy. We have no enjoyment in life. Nothing tastes good. The things that brought you pleasure previously are things to which you are now numb. It seems that when we are at our weakness moment, our spiritual enemy, the devil, tries to capitalize on our turmoil. He stirs the chaos even more with the following temptations:

DOUBT

As mentioned earlier, the devil manipulates us to doubt our relationship with the Lord. He whispers in our ears: "Why did God allow this?"; "Why does God not stop this?"; "Why does God not heal you?"; and even "Does God really care about you?"

ISOLATION

A common response to being hit in the mouth by life for most people is to turn inward and isolate themselves from others. Some do this because of shame, others because of fear, and others because they feel out of control and need solitude to regroup. Being alone has merit, until it separates you from those who will bring you loving support, from those who will speak Truth into your life, and from those who will walk through the trial with you.

ANXIETY

The enemy wants you to focus on the beating you endured rather than on the Answer. He wants you to characterize yourself as a victim instead of "fixing your eyes on Jesus" (Hebrews 12:1-3, NIV). A heart filled with anxiety has no room for peace and will therefore replace love with fear and hope with despair.

SEEK CONTROL

The conclusion many reach when their turmoil mixes doubt with isolation and anxiety is that they need to take control of their lives. Unfortunately, in doing so, they walk away from the Lord and believe the lie that life will be better if they make all the necessary decisions alone.

Hopefully, you are strong enough in the Lord to realize that the temptations you encounter during your personal drama are not viable solutions. Thankfully, the apostle Paul's strategy to winning life's battles includes Victory Action 5: Live in Peace. Peace brings order to turmoil, control to chaos, and hope to despair. The question then becomes, "How do I find peace?"

The most direct answer to finding peace in your life is to get into the presence of God. Being in God's presence changes everything! Ephesians 6:15 tells us that you can stand firm "with your feet fitted with the readiness that comes from the gospel of peace" (NIV). The normal reaction to being knocked down by the trials and temptations of life is called fight or flight response, as we have discussed in earlier chapters. Either you fight back immediately or you run away. In reality, both tactics cause you to respond in a way that your spiritual enemy wants you to respond. If you fight back, then you are acting in a manner similar to that of the devil, and you are probably doing so without an appropriate plan. If you run away, then you may avoid your problems temporarily, but eventually the problems will return and do so with greater intensity.

If you have the Gospel of Peace in your heart then you are ready, not to fight or flee, but instead to stand firm and get in God's presence. The Gospel of Peace, the Good News, is that you can stand firm knowing confidently that Jesus Christ is on your side and that He will fight your battles for you.

When I was eight years old, my family was traveling on a missions trip. Somehow, I became dehydrated and was hospitalized for a few days in Bangkok, Thailand. My memory of this event was that during the night, I was awakened by a nurse who had to put a needle in my arm for an IV. At that age, I was deadly afraid of needles and so this was very traumatic for me, especially at night, with my parents in a hotel and me alone. That the nurse could not readily find the vein in my arm only accentuated the problem. So she poked my arm with her needle numerous times before finally being successful. Needless to say, it was a very, very long night for me. While I understood that the nurse was doing the best she could, I wanted to end the torture, get out of that hospital, and go home with my family.

The next morning, the nurse woke me again for another round. Suddenly, my mom and my dad entered my room! Immediately, the torture of the situation melted and my burden was lifted! My parents were with me and I knew that everything was going to be alright.

I still had to get the IV and needed to stay in the hospital a while longer. But the game-changer was that my parents were with me, they would support and defend me, and my world was back to order as it should be. Although I could not speak the nurse's language, I remember giving her a look that said, "You are going to find my vein on the first try because my mom is watching you!"

When God enters the room, you will discover comfort, promise, power, and understanding. He restores order, brings life to the dying, and takes control of all situations immediately. During that time, we sang a song in church that has this line: "And the things of earth will grow strangely dim, in the light of His glory and grace."

Being in the presence of God returns you to your proper context. It reunites you with the One with whom you were created to be in relationship. At the very core of who you are is the fact you are created in the image of God and built to worship Him. This relationship is The Relationship; the one that matters most. When you were slammed to the canvas of life, you were knocked off-balance and out of sorts. No wonder you are dealing with anxiety, fear, and doubt! The proper response is to get back on your feet and find peace. You are still in a battle because your outward circumstances did not change. However, when you get into the presence of God, you can find amazing, inward peace that returns you to your proper context.

King David lived a vibrant and passionate life that, at times, was very traumatic and full of turmoil. Yet he understood the necessity and benefits of being in the presence of God when he wrote Psalm 23:

> The LORD is my shepherd, I shall not want. He makes me lie down in green pastures. He leads me beside still waters. He restores my soul. He leads me in paths of righteousness for his name's sake. Even though I walk through the valley of the shadow of death, I will fear no evil, for you are with me; your rod and your staff, they comfort me. You prepare a table before me in the presence of my enemies. You anoint my head with oil; my cup overflows. Surely goodness and mercy shall follow me all the days of my life, and I shall dwell in the house of the LORD forever.

In the immediate, you will find peace by devoting time to getting away, turning off the noise around you, and getting into the presence of the Lord. Take the time to read God's Word, the Bible, where God will speak to you, and meditate on it. I have found a great source of strength in reading the Psalms and the Book of Isaiah during these times as I seem to identify readily with the heart-felt nature of these books. As you read, do not be in a hurry. Allow the Truth of God's Word to wash over your heart. Consider what the

Lord is saying and talk with Him about your feelings and situation.

Often, when our lives are in turmoil, we want peace and we want it now! There may be times when you are in the presence of the Lord that solutions do not come quickly enough for you. But remember, being in God's presence and waiting on the Lord means that you are doing something and this will prove to be fruitful.

As you consider you offensive tactics in the longer term, consider that the peace you need in these moments does not come on you suddenly. In fact, all the seeds you have sown to this point will reap a harvest. Remember what you have just done! You have addressed the defensive issues, so you will not be hit again. You have adopted the offensive strategy by putting on the whole armor of God. You have determined to stand firm. You declared that you will live in truth. You will live purposely in righteousness. All these factors mixed together will result with you discovering peace. This is not a manufactured peace that crumbles at the next whiff of conflict. This is true peace, "the peace of God, which surpasses all understanding" (Philippians 4:7), and defies human logic.

> **Take the time to read God's Word, the Bible, where God will speak to you, and meditate on it. . . . Allow the Truth of God's Word to wash over your heart. Consider what the Lord is saying and talk with Him about your feelings and situation.**

There are three offensive tactics that I want you to consider as you seek to apply Victory Action 5: Live in Peace. These tactics are found in Philippians 4:4–7; "Rejoice in the Lord always; again I will say, again, rejoice. Let your reasonableness be known to everyone. The Lord is at hand; do not be anxious about anything, but in everything by prayer and supplication with thanksgiving let your requests be known to God. And the peace of God, which surpasses all understanding, will guard your hearts and your minds in Christ Jesus."

THE FIRST OFFENSIVE TACTIC THAT YOU CAN TAKE TO LIVE IN PEACE IS TO REJOICE.

The truth is that no matter how dire, depressing, and damaging the situation is that stands before you, the road to peace is paved with praise. I know when you have been hit so hard that it seems you cannot breathe, finding the strength to praise the Lord seems like a daunting task. But even if you can only muster one praise, such as "thank you that You are with me," then you are on the road to finding peace. So why do you need to rejoice, especially in the midst of your worst nightmare? I submit the following reasons:

- Praise will get you into the presence of God.
- Praise will get you focused on who is most important in your life—God.
- Praise is for your benefit! When you praise, you are aligning your life properly and allowing God to be in control.
- Praise declares that you love God more than life itself. You are not allowing the circumstances of life to dictate your relationship with God. Instead, you are allowing God to dictate the circumstances of your life.

The truth is that you have an unlimited amount of reasons why you can give praise. Here are examples of how you can praise the Lord daily:

- Praise God that He is in control. A verse that we refer to frequently is Romans 8:28: "And we know that for those who love God all things work together for good, for those who are called according to his purpose."

- Praise God that He is always with you. You can apply the promise given to Joshua: "Be strong and courageous. Do not be frightened, and do not be dismayed, for the LORD your God is with you wherever you go" (Joshua 1:9).
- Praise God that He loves you. If you were raised in church, as I was, then you will remember one of the very first verses you memorized: "For God so loved the world, that he gave his only Son, that whoever believes in him should not perish but have eternal life" (John 3:16). God loves you so much that He created you and sent His Son to die for your sins and give you freedom. Jesus willingly obeyed the Father because of His love for Him and to show His love for you.
- Praise God that your life will get better! It is because God is in control and loves you that we can stand on Romans 8:28, "And we know that for those who love God all things work together for good, for those who are called according to His purpose."

I hope that you get the point; you must praise the Lord every single day. This is a key step to living in peace.

THE SECOND OFFENSIVE TACTIC THAT YOU CAN TAKE TO LIVE IN PEACE IS TO AVOID ANXIETY.

The middle of the Philippians 4:4–7 passage states, "Do not be anxious about anything, but in everything by prayer and supplication with thanksgiving let your requests to be known to God." Anxiety is not a characteristic of God. God is not the author of anxiety, and therefore, whenever you feel anxious, you can know that this feeling is not from God. Reject anxiety and practice self-control. This exercise is a second key step to living in peace. Here are some examples of what your focus should be when you refuse to allow anxiety to grip your heart and rob your joy.

- I choose to fix my eyes on Jesus and not the situation. Jesus is with me!
- I choose my attitude based on who God is and not based on the circumstances (Habakkuk 3:16–19). The Sovereign Lord is my strength!
- I choose to live in the Truth of Jesus Christ and purpose to be righteous in my thoughts and actions. I reject the feelings of fear of the future, lack of self-worth, and uselessness. I live by God's standard!
- I choose to turn over my offender to God and allow God to judge. I am freed from this bondage!
- I choose to trust in the Lord at all times. Proverbs 3:5–6 tells me: "Trust in the LORD with all your heart, and do not lean on your own understanding. In all your ways acknowledge him, and he will make straight your paths."
- I choose to be content whatever the circumstance. Philippians 4 reveals Paul's attitude to the problems of life. This attitude is a wonderful example to us as to how we should respond to life's problems. In verses 11–13, Paul wrote, "Not that I am not speaking of being in need, for I have learned in whatever situation I am to be content. I know how to be brought low, and I know how to abound. In any and every circumstance, I have learned the secret of facing plenty and hunger, abundance and need. I can do all things through him who strengthens me."

This last sentence in the passage is one that is quoted often, "I can do all things through him who strengthens me." You hear it applied that God will give me strength to overcome overwhelming odds like winning the battle over cancer or climbing the highest mountain. Also, you hear it applied to everyday life situations, that God will give me strength to deal with difficult persons in my office. Without a doubt, God helps us through these situations, but the context of God giving us strength is that Paul has learned to be content whatever the situation.

You might be thinking that I am crazy to suggest to you that you can learn to be content in this current chapter of your personal drama. But finding Jesus in the midst of your storm and then discovering the joy of praising Him for who He is will release you from your personal prison and give you freedom to breathe again.

> But finding Jesus in the midst of your storm and then discovering the joy of praising Him for who He is will release you from your personal prison and give you freedom to breathe again.

THE THIRD OFFENSIVE TACTIC THAT YOU CAN DO TO LIVE IN PEACE IS TO COLLECT EVERYTHING THAT IS NEGATIVE IN YOUR LIFE AND HAND IT OVER TO JESUS.

Philippians 4:6 directs us to pray all kinds of prayer: "But in everything by prayer and supplication with thanksgiving let your requests be made known to God." We are going to discuss the importance and power of prayer in a subsequent chapter but for now, I implore you to stop carrying your heavy burden and give it over to Jesus in prayer. Trust Him. He can handle any, and all, of your trials, disappointments, doubts, and fears. He is the One who will balance the scales of justice and bring you redemption.

What will happen when you reach out daily to God in praise, as you determine to reject anxiety, and as you give your burdens to Him? Philippians 4:7 gives us the result: "And the peace of God, which surpasses all understanding, will guard your hearts and your minds in Christ Jesus." Peace! Perfect peace! Peace that surpasses all understanding!

Peace will give you hope. Peace will give you confidence that your situation will change and that one day you will thrive again.

Peace will give you hope. Peace will give you confidence that your situation will change and that one day you will thrive again. Peace brings a sense of normalcy into your life and calms your heart and spirit.

When you live in the Gospel of Peace, then you are fitted with the readiness to stand firm, and to move according to God's plan for your life instead of being tossed chaotically on the waves of life's storms. You can react confidently to life's problems because of the One to whom you belong. You belong to Jesus! He said in John 14:27, "Peace I leave with you; my peace I give to you. Not as the world gives do I give to you. Let not your hearts be troubled, neither let them be afraid."

FOR YOU TO CONSIDER

1. Identify how the following temptations may be impacting your life right now: doubt, isolation, anxiety, and seeking control.

2. One avenue to peace is to rejoice. List ten praises that you should give to the Lord today.

3. A second response to temptation is to avoid anxiety. List two of the examples provided that you know you must apply in order to find peace. Then write what your action points will be in response.

4. In your mind, gather all that is negative in your life and hand it over the Jesus. Pray John 14:27 as a personal prayer: "Peace I leave with you; my peace I give to you. Not as the world gives do I give to you. Let not your hearts be troubled, neither let them be afraid."

SCRIPTURE FOR YOU TO PRAY TODAY

"Do not be anxious about anything, but in everything, by prayer and supplication with thanksgiving let your requests be made known to God. And the peace of God, which surpasses all understanding, will guard your hearts and your minds in Christ Jesus" (Philippians 4:6–7).

What is the Lord saying to you right now?

VICTORY ACTION 6

LIVE IN FAITH

YOUR BELIEFS ARE YOUR STRENGTH

"In all circumstances take up the shield of faith, with which you can extinguish all the flaming darts of the evil one."

EPHESIANS 6:16

"As the Scriptures tell us, 'Anyone who trusts in him will never be disgraced.'"

ROMANS 10:11, NLT

The perfect life that he worked to build so diligently and strategically was about to be shattered into a million pieces. Truthfully, it was not his fault. It really did not matter as to what brought him to this point, be it a betrayal of relationship, loss of employment, or a life-threatening report from the doctor. What matters at this very moment is the decision he is about to make. Will he listen to the voices of doom? Will he attempt to overcome by thinking positive thoughts and going it alone? Or is there another way?

Fortunately for him, he remembered the lessons about God that he learned in Sunday School. Lessons like "God will never leave you or forsake you," and the Bible verse telling him to trust in the Lord with all his heart. He decides, at that very moment, that he is going full in—100 percent—and follow God, then allow the chips to fall where they may. Either God will protect and defend him, or God is a myth. But in his heart he knows that this is more than a Hail Mary pass or a risky proposition. God is real. God is his friend—especially in his time of need. He determines to press forward with God by his side. Later, he would look back at this moment and tell his children that what could have been the tipping point to personal destruction, instead propelled him to victory. It was due to one simple word; faith.

I would like to tell you that at this point in your journey, the difficult part of rebuilding your life is over. But that would not be the truth. Experience tells us that our spiritual enemy, the devil, will continue to take the fight to you. He has knocked you down to the canvas of life. You have responded in the ways that we have discussed so far and you are standing firm. He is now ready to hit you again! He is going to test you and see if you really have a fight in you. What is different this time though is that you are ready to defend yourself and to respond offensively.

Paul instructs us in Ephesians 6:16, "In addition to all this, take up the shield of faith, with which you can extinguish all the flaming arrows of the evil one." This is what we will call Victory Action 6:

Live in Faith.

While you are gaining momentum to a victorious life, you can expect the evil one to attack you. The devil will do everything he can to scare you, to intimidate you, and to cause you to doubt, fear, be anxious, isolated, and quit on life. His response will be dramatic and impressive, like fiery arrows filling the sky to descend on defenseless victims. But he can only impact you negatively if you take your eyes off Jesus and focus on his attacks.

> **Faith is the belief in God so strong that you will stand with Him no matter what. This is what you need to understand: When you live by faith, your beliefs in God are your strength.**

Earlier, I told you that you can expect the attacks of the enemy to return like ocean waves pounding the beach shore. But when you respond with truth, righteousness, and peace, and the attacks return, remember that you are still in God's hands, His will, and His plans. The apostle Paul told us, "in all circumstances" or "in every situation" (HCSB) take up the shield of faith. In Hebrews 12:1–3, Paul instructed us,

Therefore, since we are surrounded by so great cloud of witnesses, let us also lay off every weight, and sin that clings so closely, and let us run with endurance the race that is set out for us, looking to Jesus, the founder and perfecter of our faith, who for the joy that was set before him endured the cross, despising the shame, and is seated at the right hand of the throne of God. Consider him who endured from sinners, such hostility against himself, so that you may not grow weary and fainthearted.

You can see the arrows of the enemy extinguished by standing firm behind the "shield of faith." So what is faith? Faith is the belief in God so strong that you will stand with Him no matter what. This is what you need to understand: When you live by faith, your beliefs in God are your strength. Regardless of the current circumstances, regardless of what people around you are saying, and regardless even in the face of the loss of hope, you will stand with God! Your hope is in the Lord. Your assurance of victory is in the Lord. Hebrews 11:1 puts it this way: "Now faith is assurance of things hoped for, the conviction of things not seen." You may not see an immediate solution to your life issue or be avenged for the wrongs done to you. But like a farmer who plants seed in one season, works the fields, and anticipates the season of an abundant harvest, you can stand firm with the shield of faith knowing that you will be protected now and be assured that victory will come.

Allow me to make some suggestions how you can live in faith personally and collectively. You can respond in faith personally by allowing your belief in God to be your strength. You can respond in faith collectively, and by that, I mean that you situate yourself strategically around people who love the Lord, who will speak Truth into your life. Both of these responses will develop your faith in the Lord.

There are many ways that you can respond personally in faith during your personal drama that will protect you and draw you closer to God. I want to begin this aspect of our discussion by reminding you of the story in 1 Samuel 17 that you learned as a child: David and Goliath.

The nation of Israel was in a battle with the Philistines. They determined that one representative from each army would face off in battle with the winner take all. This was well and good until the Philistines revealed that their warrior was a giant. Even the mighty soldiers of Israel were paralyzed by fear for they believed Goliath to be unbeatable. If know the story, you know it took the faith of a young man, some say even a boy, to defeat the undefeatable, to bring victory to Israel, and glory to God.

David's belief in God was his strength. His five actions during this account are valuable lessons for us as we "take up the shield of faith" before our offender. His response in the face of death serves as a road map for us to follow so we can overcome the attacks of our spiritual enemy.

FIRST, LOOK AT YOUR PERSONAL DRAMA FROM GOD'S PERSPECTIVE.

The army of Israel saw Goliath as a state-of-the-art killing machine who was too big to overcome, but David saw him as a giant who was too big to miss. After David surveyed the situation and placed it into proper perspective, he asked, "Who is this uncircumcised Philistine, that he should defy the armies of the living God?" (1 Samuel 17:26). That simple statement refocused the power and authority from the enemy—a negative faith if you will— to the One who is truly in control of everything in

What was meant to be a season of destruction to you, God will use as a season of victory, showing you His power and glory.

heaven and earth, and He is God. What was meant to be a season of destruction to you, God will use as a season of victory, showing you His power and glory.

Right now, faith means that your belief in God is your strength. Do you really think that God was surprised by your drama? I guarantee that no matter what trial may be, God has seen it before and brought people through to victory. Do you really believe that He will leave you in the very moment that you need Him the most? Of course not! Your belief in God was designed for this. Turn to him now. Later, David would write, "Even though I walk through the valley of the shadow of death, I will fear no evil, for you are with me; your rod and staff, they comfort me" (Psalm 23:4). By faith, you can declare in your heart that you will walk with God and know that this will "extinguish all the flaming darts of the evil one" (Ephesians 6:16). Your faith in God that defines the battle from His perspective is your strength.

SECOND, REMEMBER THAT GOD IS FAITHFUL.

David's proclamation of faith in God was a tremendous breath of life into the army of Israel. Immediately, he was brought before King Saul as a potential defender of the nation. What Saul saw though was a mere youth who was not battle tested. He believed that sending David before Goliath was sending him to a quick and horrible death. But David's reply to the King is our example of faith under fire: he remembered the victories of the past given to him by God. "Your servant has struck down both lions and the bears, and this uncircumcised Philistine shall be like one of them, for he has defied the armies of the living God. . . . The LORD who delivered me from the paw of the lion and the paw of the bear will deliver me from the hand of this Philistine" (1 Samuel 17:36–37).

> Remember the victories that God has brought you! Remember how He saved and protected you. . . . He is still the same!

While David had never encountered an enemy of such physical prowess and magnitude, his faith in God was developed in his short life through the victories he experienced when attacked previously. The common thread in David's recounting of the past was the faithfulness of God.

In the same way, remember the victories that God has brought you! Remember how He saved and protected you. Remember how He brought people into your life who walked with you and helped make you a better person. He is still the same! Maybe the obstacle before you is new to you. But God was faithful to others who encountered that same issue and brought them through, and He will do the same for you.

By faith, you can declare that God will bring you victory. Instead of aligning your heart with the fear of the attacks by the enemy, you can focus the totality of who you are on the Lord. Your faith in God to believe that He is faithful is your strength.

THIRD, FIGHT THE BATTLE GOD'S WAY.

King Saul dressed David in his armor in preparation for battle. On one hand, this was admirable because a good general must equip his soldiers with the best equipment possible. On the other hand, Saul did this on the very slim chance that David should win the battle, then Saul could claim victory, because David was wearing the King's armor! But as we read in 1 Samuel 17:39–40, David refused the armor as he was not used to it and instead chose five smooth stones for his sling and approached the Philistine. If victory would be achieved that day, there would be no doubt that it came from the Lord.

By faith, your implicit trust in the Lord is your strength. Proverbs 3:5–6 give us wise instruction, "Trust in the LORD with all your heart, and do not lean on your own understanding. In all your ways, acknowledge Him and He will make straight your paths." As we have been leading up to in previous chapters together, fighting the battle God's way means that you will live daily, by faith, the fulfillment of this Proverbs passage.

What can the enemy do to you if you respond by trusting in the Lord? He will shoot the flaming arrow of anxiety, but you trust in the Lord and will find His peace. He will throw the shroud of depression on you, but your trust in the Lord will bring you joy. He will force the logic of your situation to get you to accept that your position on the canvas of life is your new home, but your trust in the Lord will fill your heart with hope.

I pray that you are not giving serious thought now to taking control of the situation instead of giving it over to God. Proverbs counsels us to "not lean on your own understanding." This is the very situation in which you need to submit your will to the Lord and follow Him. He alone will lead you out of the fog of life and into the Light. He alone removes the obstacles before you and brings order to the chaos. If God is out of the conversation, then the devil can deceive you, fool you, and use worldly logic against you. But what can he do to you when your response is, "This does not make sense to me, but I am going to trust in the Lord no matter what happens"?

How can the devil respond to you when you give praise to God constantly for His love and thank Him daily for another opportunity to serve Him? When you acknowledge God in all your ways, He will set your crooked path straight. This means that He will right the wrong, bring order to your chaos, and overcome your doubts and depression with peace and joy. Be rid of the enemy's bondage and replace it with the freedom of believing—without reservations—that God is on your side, and therefore, He is in control and has your very best interest at heart. Your faith in God to believe that you must fight the battle God's way is your strength.

FOURTH, REMEMBER THAT GOD FIGHTS FOR YOU!

David stood before Goliath and the entire Philistine army and made a public declaration of faith, "That all this assembly may know that the LORD saves not with sword and spear. For the battle is the

LORD's, and he will give you into our hand." (1 Samuel 17:47). Just as "the battle is the LORD's" for David, the Lord is battling for you! It would seem appropriate to add, "and the Lord never loses!" but that would imply that He has an opponent who has the potential, however large or small, of defeating Him.

The truth is no one in heaven, on earth, or anywhere else can oppose God. So when you determine to stand with Him, you become automatically the winner and in the majority. David wrote, "The LORD is on my side; I will not fear. What can man do to me?" (Psalm 118:6). Paul wrote in Romans 8:31–39:

> *What then shall we say to these things? If God is for us, who can be against us? He who did not spare his own Son but gave him up for us all, how will he not also with him graciously give us all things? Who shall bring any charge against God's elect? It is God who justifies. Who is to condemn? Christ Jesus is the one who died—more than that, who was raised—who is at the right hand of God, who indeed is interceding for us. Who shall separate us from the love of Christ? Shall tribulation, or distress, or persecution, or famine, or nakedness, or danger, or sword? As it is written: "For your sake we are bing killed all day long; we are regarded as sheep to be slaughtered." No, in all these things we are more than conquerors through him who loved us. For I am sure that neither death nor life, nor angels nor rulers, nor things present nor things to come, nor powers, nor height nor depth, nor anything else in all creation, will be able to separate us from the love of God in Christ Jesus our Lord.*

The devil will use every tactic in his arsenal to cause you to fear and to doubt. Your best response is to stand with the Lord and declare to the enemy, "If you have a problem with me then take it up with the Lord!" End of story! Your faith in God to believe that He fights for you is your strength.

FIFTH, DO WHAT YOU ARE SUPPOSED TO DO!

When Goliath moved closer to attack David, what did the young man do? Did he drop his sling and run away? Did he look back to the King for assurance that he was doing what was right? First Samuel 17:48 tells us that, "David ran quickly toward the battle line to meet the Philistine." David then slung the stone, hit the giant in the forehead, and killed him instantly. He then ran and stood over the dead body. He took Goliath's own sword and cut off his head, leaving no doubt that the Lord brought the victory to Israel through His servant.

In the same way, you must do what you should. Your assignment right now is to have the faith in God to know that your beliefs are your strength. Remember that Hebrews 11:1 instructs us, "Now faith is the assurance of things hope for, the conviction of things not seen." You are trusting in the Lord to bring you the victory even though at this moment all you see is your life in shambles. You believe that God is faithful even though the voices around you shout that you have been abandoned. But even in the worst of times, you can be certain of what you hope for because you are standing with the One who is faithful.

And as you stand in faith, you must keep the end result in focus and act accordingly. You are not adrift on the sea of doubt and chaos. You have a plan now which you can follow with purpose and see the Lord bring the desired outcome. This is what Paul meant when he wrote, "We look not to the things that are seen but to the things that are unseen. For the things that are seen are transient, but the things that are unseen are eternal" (2 Corinthians 4:18).

You do not have to give in to the temptation to respond to your troubles in a manner similar to the way your offender hurt you. This is short-sighted and will not bring you your desired result. Instead, you must respond by focusing on the eternal, the end result, and then live in a manner that glorifies the Lord. You must respond by fighting by God's rules and avoid lowering yourself to the tactics of your offender. Keep focused on your identity, for you belong to God, and on your desired outcome which is victory without regrets. Determine in your heart that you will not allow the obstacle of the immediate rob you of your eternal reward.

Keep focused on your identity, for you belong to God, and on your desired outcome which is victory without regrets. Determine in your heart that you will not allow the obstacle of the immediate rob you of your eternal reward.

Any athlete of substance will know, you cannot give in or give up when training is tough or the game is not going your way. Instead, you must keep focused at all times on the end game and that is winning. The joy of victory will far exceed the trials of the battle and so you press on, fixing your eyes on the ultimate prize.

Remember that before the greatest reward comes your greatest trial. You can never experience the greatest comeback in your life if you quit before attempting to overcome seemingly insurmountable odds. And you can only know if your faith in God has meaning when you are tested.

Anyone can look at your situation and become depressed and robbed of joy. But you have been equipped to stand firm in faith next to the Lord and focus on the ultimate victory that only He can bring. So respond in a manner that honors God. Live and fight by His rules. Allow the impending victory to fuel you to respond rightly and to navigate you expertly through the current season of obstacles.

You can fix your eyes on the unseen because you are standing with the Lord. The account in 2 Kings 6 of how a king tried to abduct the prophet Elisha provides us with a good example of the unseen. The king's army with horses and chariots surrounded the city where Elisha and his servant stayed. When the servant saw the imposing enemy, he panicked. But Elisha calmed his servant by saying, "Do not be afraid, for those who are with us are more than those who are with them" (2 Kings 6:16). Elisha prayed for the Lord to open the servant's eyes and he saw that the hills were full of horses and chariots of fire about them. The victory was assured! The servant was focused initially on the seen, but God opened his eyes to see the unseen. I pray that God will open your eyes and heart to know that He is with you and fighting for you this very moment.

You must do what you know to do: focus on the desired outcome and act in the appropriate manner to get there. Your faith to do what you must do is your strength.

We have just considered that you can respond in faith personally by allowing your belief in God to be your strength. Now, you should know that another way that you can "put up the shield of faith" and thwart the attacks of the enemy is to consider your faith in God in context with the family of God, the Church. There is no need for you to stand firm alone and hold the shield of faith. There are plenty of other believers who are engaged in the very same battle.

Ecclesiastes 4:12 says, "Though a man might prevail against

one who is alone, two can withstand him—a threefold cord is not quickly broken." There are people in the family of God who, by the grace of God, have overcome your life issue. Allow them to stand with you, encourage you, speak God's Truth into your life, protect you, and to help you in tangible ways.

I may need to remind you that this strategy makes four basic assumptions. First, it assumes that you will put aside your pride and admit that you need help. Second, it assumes that you will be open to hearing God's Truth and allow it to penetrate your heart. Third, it assumes that you will make whatever changes are needed; spiritually, socially, emotionally, psychologically, physically, and materially. Fourth, it assumes that you will allow people that the Lord brings into your life to travel this portion of life's journey with you. These can be very large assumptions but they are issues that you must address. Placing yourself in the context of the family of God is another way of taking up the shield of faith.

> There are people in the family of God who, by the grace of God, have overcome your life issue. Allow them to stand with you, encourage you, speak God's Truth into your life, protect you, and to help you in tangible ways.

When I experienced my personal drama and was knocked to the canvas of life, the Lord brought people to me who were life-savers and difference-makers. While not many of them continue in my personal journey today, they were present and breathed life into me at just the right time—when I needed them the most. Some stood with me and just listened. Some were people who had endured great personal tragedy and were an example to me of how faith in God brought them through. Some spoke God's Truth into my life. Some protected me from bad attitudes, from doing something stupid like retaliate, and from the voices of doubt during my weak moments. Some prepared meals for me, took me to a ball game to give me a moment of relief, and even helped me learn to laugh again. All of these people, I believe, were directed by God to enter my life by God at the very moment that I needed their special gifts the most. I am forever grateful for their willingness to stand with me in the faith and be my friend. This can be your story, too!

So how do we live our faith in our daily walk? Daily, you can proclaim loudly that your faith is in God alone. This will be your strength and extinguish those fiery arrows meant to destroy you. Here are examples of what you can believe every day. You can have faith that:

- God is in control.
- God will balance the scales of justice.
- God will vindicate you.
- God will provide.
- God will give you the strength to endure during this trial.
- "And we know that for those who love God all things work together for good, for those who are called according to his purpose" (Romans 8:28).
- God will bring people into your life to stand with you.
- There will be better days.
- God will get the glory through this season of your bleakest season of life.

FOR YOU TO CONSIDER

1. What is your definition of faith and what must you do to live by faith?

2. Look at your personal drama from God's perspective and explain how His presence will change your situation.

3. List at least three accounts in your life when God was faithful.

4. What changes must you make to fight the battle God's way?

5. What does this phrase, "we are more than conquerors" (Romans 8:37), mean to you?

6. What must you do in response to your current situation and as you remember that God is with you at all times?

7. Who is standing with you from the family of God?

8. The chapter ends with examples of what you can believe every day. Personalize each one in a prayer.

SCRIPTURE FOR YOU TO PRAY TODAY

"Trust in the LORD with all your heart, and do not lean on your own understanding. In all your ways acknowledge Him, and He will make straight paths" (Proverbs 3:3–5).

What is the Lord saying to you right now?

VICTORY ACTION 7

LIVE IN HOPE

HOPE KEEPS YOUR LIFE VIBRANT

"And take the helmet of salvation."

EPHESIANS 6:17A

"May the God of hope fill you with all joy and peace as you trust in him, so that you may overflow with hope by the power of the Holy Spirit."

ROMANS 15:13

The aroma of ethnic food made my heart jump as I walked into the restaurant that Tuesday night. I knew that I was in for a culinary delight! It was early in the evening, and yet the room was filled with people seated at the tables. They were in different stages of their dining experience; some were ordering, some waiting for their food, some were in deep conversation, and not a few were on their cell phones, neglecting the others at their table. If you had asked me what the common factor was for everyone at the restaurant, I would have been correct if I responded that they were all hungry and wanting something to eat. But there was another commonality that was much deeper and more meaningful.

At the table next to the mural on the wall was a man who sat alone and stared at his plate as if he was the only person in the room. His reality was that he was three months into his unemployment after being laid off because his company "right sized" due to their financial mismanagement. His personal emergency fund for such a moment was drained dry and the remainder of his savings evaporated. He had no idea how he could meet his mortgage, pay for his son's upcoming college tuition, or even how to pay the bills this month. Sadly, his self-image and self-worth took a tremendous hit and caused him to plunge into a personal downward spiral. He could see no rescue coming; he had lost all hope.

The truth was that many of the people in the restaurant that night were dealing with such overwhelming issues that they too had lost all hope. The woman seated with her family by the spiced tea dispenser knew that her husband's infidelity was tearing apart their relationship. She lost hope that they would ever love each other again. Even the waiter was in personal crises because his grandmother, who raised him after his parents were killed in a car accident, was in a life-threatening coma. He lost hope of ever speaking to her again.

If indeed hope is the "oxygen of the soul," then these people were participating in their last supper. Outwardly, they seemed like any other people that night. Inwardly, they were defeated and lost their will to fight. Hope was gone.

As we begin this portion of our journey together, let us consider why it is vital, and timely, to "take the helmet of salvation" as instructed by the apostle Paul in Ephesians 6:17. It seems to me that the use of the helmet implies that we must protect our minds, the place where we think, reason, develop and exercise our will, and choose to do what is right over and against our emotions. We tend to picture the heart as the seat of our emotions while those in other cultures use other body parts to make a similar analogy.

When life knocks you down and you are at your most vulnerable, you must allow yourself time to feel the pain, to grieve, and to express your emotions. But you cannot stay there! You must muster as much self-discipline as you can and choose to turn your eyes to Jesus. Choosing to turn to Jesus means that you will trust Him without reservation. Like Joshua, you must declare, "As for me and my house, we will serve the Lord" (Joshua 24:15).

The moment you focus on Jesus is the very moment that salvation embraces you and frees you from the bondage of your personal dilemma. Jesus is the Answer. In Him, there is life, love, promise, future, purpose, healing, freedom, and hope. Jesus gives you hope for today that you will not only survive, but that you can begin building today your life for tomorrow. Jesus gives you hope for your future that there are indeed brighter days ahead—days of fulfillment and days of victory. Jesus gives you hope for eternity, because we have life after death and that will be so amazing that we cannot begin to comprehend what it will be like!

So I am equating the helmet of salvation with Victory Action 7: Live in Hope. When you live in salvation, you have hope because you know the One to whom you belong, Jesus. Your past is forgiven. He will journey with you in your present and give you a future that is beyond belief. First Thessalonians 5:8 reveals the relationship between hope and salvation as well, "Since we belong to the day, let us be sober, having put on the breastplate of faith and love, and for a helmet the hope of salvation."

I believe that if you have been reading this book in the order from the beginning, then you have discovered the joy of rebuilding a vibrant life filled with hope! But if you came immediately to this chapter because you are seeking desperately to reconnect with hope, then you need to know that your hope is found in Jesus Christ and that you must focus the entirety of your being on Him!

> **Living by faith taught us to believe in God, no matter what! Living by hope teaches us to have the attitude to trust in God, no matter what!**

Victory Action 7: Live in Hope is not just re-created in your heart, but it provides a new living hope that will heal the wounds of the past, empower you for today, and inspire you to move forward in confidence as you march toward a promising future. Paul wrote that now is the time for you to "take the helmet of salvation" (Ephesians 6:17). While your life-crushing defeat may have left you feeling overwhelmed emotionally, Paul's instruction will empower you to take control of your thoughts, to focus on the victory that Christ has won, and to respond to life with confidence. Living by faith taught us to believe in God, no matter what! Living by hope teaches us to have the attitude to trust in God, no matter what!

Paul's prayer in Romans 15:13 provides the recipe to finding hope and your part of this salvation equation depends on your willingness to trust in Him: "May the God of hope fill you with all joy and peace in believing, so that by the power of the Holy Spirit you may abound in hope." Will you trust in God right now that He will get you off the canvas of life's troubles, that He will bring healing to your heart, and that He will bring the Light of His love into very core of your darkest hour?

As we discussed earlier, who else will you trust? Will you trust your ability to overcome? Will you trust the counsel of others? Will you seek wisdom from a worldview, a political ideology, or religious teaching that takes you away from Christ? Even if your defeat has crushed your hope and stomped out your will to fight, the first step to your salvation is to declare that you will trust implicitly in God. Remember that such a declaration means that you will live and fight by His rules, submit to His authority, and serve Him for His glory. This is not the time for you to walk away from your relationship with the Lord; this is the time to embrace Him fully!

Trust the Lord that He will do the following:

- He will position you to breathe again!
- He will cover you with His love acceptance and forgiveness.
- He will instill again in you a feeling of significance and purpose.
- He will take that which was meant for evil and turn it into good, all for His glory.

Trusting in the Lord will alter your view of the world and can transform the most negative person into a God-optimist; one whose attitude is to follow God even in spite of the circumstances. An attitude that is focused on trusting in the Lord will impact even your prayers.

Let's say that you are a parent whose eldest daughter is away relationally from the Lord. It is so easy to focus on what she is doing wrong, how she is missing the opportunity to fulfill her potential, and what you perceive to be the inevitable outcomes of her current behavior. Naturally, you will spend countless hours crying out to the Lord for His intervention. If you are not careful, though, your unanswered prayers can lead you to worry, which leads to anxiety, which leads to bitterness, and could even see you walk away from the Lord. Instead, determine in your head and in your heart that your attitude will be one that honors God. Live in hope!

Trusting the Lord at all times transforms your prayers from anxiety and doubt to hope and victory. Living in Hope means that you can pray for your prodigal like this:

- Lord, I thank you that you love my child more than I do.
- I thank you that you leave the ninety-nine sheep who are in the open country to find the one sheep which is lost (see Matthew 18:10–14).
- I thank you that you are not willing that anyone will perish but that you want every single person to be in right relationship with you (see 2 Peter 3:9).
- I thank you that you will bring people into my child's life to speak truth to her, to challenge her to live rightly, and model your love.
- I thank you that this could be the day that the prodigal returns.
- Help me to never grow weary of praying, loving, and expecting the best of her.

Such prayers are grounded in the truth of your child's waywardness, yet they are focused on the One who loves all and who makes all things new: Jesus Christ. Your trust will be rewarded with joy and peace, even when the circumstances declare that you are suffering depression and chaos. The Holy Spirit then enters your arena and empowers you to stand firm and to be filled in abundance with hope.

Living in hope is an amazing place to be! You understand completely the severity of your current quagmire, and yet the helmet of salvation elevates your heart's affections, mind's attention, and resulting behaviors to see Jesus. Our Lord was never baffled, stumped, or caught unaware or unprepared. He knew the will of the Father and was obedient to death, even death on the cross. When you follow Christ and His example, you will then be empowered by the Holy Spirit to thrive in the rarefied air of living in hope and victory.

Living in hope will cause you to obey God to the point of seeming to be out of touch with your circumstances, arrogant, or even nonsensical to those who do not know Him. But living in hope means that you know at the end of the contest, you are on the winning team! Here are some examples of people mentioned in God's Word to inspire you to live in hope.

> **When you follow Christ and His example, you will then be empowered by the Holy Spirit to thrive in the rarefied air of living in hope and victory.**

NOAH

The Bible says that Noah was a righteous man who found favor in God's eyes. God declared that He would destroy humanity and the earth by a flood because of their violence and wickedness. Before the rains came, it probably seemed quite odd to Noah's neighbors, and even to his friends and family, that he was building a boat to save his family from global destruction. No doubt, he endured brutal ridicule for his willingness to be obedient to God when his actions were beyond the conventional reason of the day. Yet Noah lived in hope that God was faithful and that His will would be done. And he "did all that God commanded him," (Genesis 6:22).

As the Sunday School song goes, "the rains came down and the floods when up," and Noah's hope in God become reality!

ABRAHAM

God commanded Abram and Sarai to move to a distant land they had never seen and live among a people they had never met. God promised Abram that he would be the father of many nations. Humanly speaking, this was an outrageous outcome since Abram and Sarai were well beyond the years of child bearing, much less having the desire and strength to raise all those children! In the process of being obedient to God, their names were changed and they lived under God's covenant. They did migrate to a new land and they lived among a different people.

They hit some speed bumps along the way, like the time Abraham grew impatient with God's plan and fathered a child that was not with Sarah. But Abraham lived in the hope that God's will would be done. He was faithful to do what God told him to do because, "he was looking forward to the city that has foundations, whose designer and builder is God" (Hebrews 11:10). In the end, Abraham's hope in God became reality!

MOSES

Moses was a late bloomer in life who focused on his physical limitations and emotional baggage. God encountered him and tasked him with the role of leading His children out of bondage from the world's greatest superpower of that day. There were doubts and fears and periods of loneliness for Moses during this incredible journey. But through it all, he lived in hope that God was faithful to see His will be done. When they needed direction, God provided a cloud by day for them to follow and a pillar of fire by night. When they needed to rid themselves of their captors, God sent the destroyer to kill the firstborn of the Egyptians and then separated the Red Sea so the Israelites could escape to safety. When they were dying of thirst, God instructed Moses to strike the rock and water gushed out like a river. When they were in dire need of bread and meat to eat, God miraculously provided manna six days a week and had quail fly in to sustain them. Moses' hope in God became reality as He led His children to the land flowing with milk and honey!

These three leaders lived in hope! They devoted their lives to trusting God, to obeying Him, and to be faithful and righteous. I am inspired also by the biblical accounts of individuals who were so immersed in living in hope that their confidence in the Lord bordered on spiritual arrogance! Here are some examples:

THREE HEBREW YOUNG MEN

Shadrach, Meshach, and Abednego were three Hebrew captives who rose to attain leadership positions in the Babylonian Empire. They were commanded to bow before a golden image of King Nebuchadnezzar as a sign of worship or they would be killed. So their choices were insult God by worshiping a false god or die. This was a defining moment in their lives, to state it mildly!

They loved God so much, and they lived in the hope of their salvation so deeply, that they stood before the king and stated, "O Nebuchadnezzar, we have no need to answer you in this matter. If this be so, our God whom we serve is able to deliver us from the burning fiery furnace, and he will deliver us out of your hand, O king. *But if not, be it known to you, O king, that we will not serve your gods or worship the golden image that you have set up*'" (Daniel 3:16–18, emphasis added). Such confidence! Such arrogance! One cannot talk to a king in that manner and expect to live!

King Nebuchadnezzar was so enraged that he ordered the furnace to be heated seven times hotter than usual. The three young men were tied and thrown into the fiery furnace. To the amazement of the king, the three were not alone in the fire! In fact, a fourth man was there, walking unbound and unharmed and looked "like a son of the gods" (Daniel 3:25). Many scholars believe the fourth man was Jesus.

The three young men emerged from the fiery furnace completely unharmed. Their hair was not singed, their robes were not scorched, and there was no smell of fire on them! King Nebuchadnezzar then praised the God of Shadrach, Meshach, and Abednego and declared that anyone who opposed their God would be "torn limb from limb, and their houses laid in ruins, for there is no other god is able to rescue in this way!" (Daniel 3:29).

The unabashed confidence in the Lord led to their salvation and impacted greatly on how the Babylonians viewed the true God. The young men are our example of how living in hope is the only way to live!

THE DISCIPLES

The Book of Acts shares the incredible account of how believers accepted Christ's command to take the Good News into all the world. They faced extreme hardships, cruelty, and persecution regularly. Yet they were unshaken in their resolve to live in hope. One example of this was when the disciples were thrown into jail for preaching and healing people. The religious leaders of the day were jealous and did their best to terminate their ministry. In Acts 5, we read that the Lord opened the doors of the jail, released the disciples, and told them, "Go and stand in the temple and speak to the people all the words of this Life" (Acts 5:20).

The disciples obeyed and quickly found themselves standing before the High Priest and the Sanhedrin; the important leaders of their nation. Humanly speaking, this situation was not one that would end well for the disciples. The odds of them being physically tortured within an inch of their lives were enormous. They could be thrown out of the temple permanently and their families ostracized forever. Their actions to follow Christ could cause their family name to be erased permanently from the annals of their nation. Yet they stood in front of all the religious leaders, knowing full well the implications of their actions and attitudes, and declared, "We must obey God rather than men!" (Acts 5:29). What confidence in the Lord!

We would like to think that the Jewish religious leaders, like King Nebuchadnezzar, were so impressed by their words that they praised God and released the disciples. Instead, the disciples were flogged and ordered to cease speaking "in the name of Jesus" (Acts 5:40). But did the disciples become depressed and doubt their calling? Did they question why God did not intervene when they were being beaten? Check out their response:

"[The apostles] left the presence of the council, *rejoicing that they were counted worthy to suffer dishonor for the name*. And every day, in the temple and from house to house, they did not cease teaching and preaching the good news that the Christ is Jesus" (Acts 5:41–42, emphasis added). They rejoiced because they had been counted worthy of suffering disgrace for the Name! What an amazing example of living in hope of their salvation!

The disciples were not rejoicing because they suffered, but because their suffering identified them with Jesus. Their hearts were ripped apart like tearing flesh from bone and their dreams utterly and completely crushed when their Savior and Lord was tortured and crucified on the cross. We cannot imagine the depth of their despair during this time of seemingly shocking defeat. But Jesus was not down for the count! The grave could not hold him and He rose again on the third day to defeat sin and death.

Just as Jesus was obedient to the will of the Heavenly Father to the point of suffering death, the disciples knew that they too would endure suffering because they were following in the footsteps of their Master. At the same time, the victory that Christ brought to defeat sin is the same victory that He would bring to His disciples to overcome suffering in His Name. It makes sense then that they had to obey God rather than men!

> **Jesus Christ provides our salvation for every dilemma, every season of life, and in every moment of our journey. We can live in full confidence in the Lord!**

This is the realm in which we should each live! We must live in hope! Jesus Christ provides our salvation for every dilemma, every season of life, and in every moment of our journey. We can live in full confidence in the Lord!

As you stand firm, you must remember to take the helmet of salvation. You no longer have to be bound by fear from the attacks of your spiritual enemy. Your external circumstances do not dictate your internal self-talk because you can trust in the Lord. You are freed from the feelings of not being in control of your life because you can trust in the Lord. He will then fill you with such joy and peace that you will overflow with hope by the power of the Holy Spirit.

Walk in the hope of your salvation.

Dream in the hope of your salvation.

Fulfill God's destiny for your life in the hope of your salvation!

FOR YOU TO CONSIDER

1. What must you do to "walk in the hope of your salvation"?

2. What are your dreams for the future as you follow the Lord?

3. What does God want you to do and what steps should you take toward seeing His will accomplished in your life?

SCRIPTURE FOR YOU TO PRAY TODAY

"May the God of hope fill you with all joy and peace as you trust in him, so that you may overflow with hope by the power of the Holy Spirit" (Romans 15:13).

What is the Lord saying to you right now?

VICTORY ACTION 8

LIVE IN THE WORD OF GOD

THE BIBLE IS THE FOUNDATION OF YOUR LIFE

*"And take . . . the sword of the Spirit, which
is the word of God."*

EPHESIANS 6:17B

*"For the word of God is alive and active. Sharper
than any double-edged sword, it penetrates even
to dividing soul and spirit, joints and marrow; it
judges the thoughts and attitudes of the heart."*

HEBREWS 4:12

The mass murderer who terrorized the state for over two decades as "the most prolific serial killer in American history" now sat in the court room listening to the families of his victims. They expressed their feelings and emotions to him as part of their healing process. Their pain, anger, and hurt spewed without reservation and in no uncertain terms. They wanted the killer to suffer even more than he had hurt their loved ones. They wanted no mercy or leniency. In fact, one person declared that she hoped he died a painful and tortured death. The killer sat listening to them and responded with a deadpan, dispassionate, and detached stare. It seemed that no words, no emotion, and no pain expressed could penetrate his cold stare and hardened heart.

Then, a man came to the podium and spoke with a different tone in his voice. He stated an entirely different message. As I watched this live on TV, I sensed that this man was unlike those who spoke before him. With pain in his voice, he spoke slowly, measuring his words with controlled passion, and directly to the killer who had shown no mercy to his daughter. "There are people here who hate you. I am not one of them. You have made it difficult to live up to what I believe and that is what God says to do. And that is to forgive. You are forgiven, sir."

I will never forget the mass murder's response! He was unfazed by the anger and hatred expressed previously. But now, he broke into tears when encountered by the love of God displayed by the mourning father. Repaying evil with evil did not penetrate the hardened heart, but it was God's Word displayed in love that brought an outward expression of remorse. For that one moment, the killer encountered the Truth of God's Word and saw himself truly for who he was.

It is interesting to me that the apostle Paul used two pieces of a soldier's armor in the same sentence when he wrote, "Take the helmet of salvation, and the sword of the Spirit, which is the word of God" (Ephesians 6:17). In order to live in the hope of your salvation, you need to fill your heart and mind with the Truth of God's Word. Working simultaneously with Victory Action 7: Live in Hope is Victory Action 8: Live in the Word of God.

The Word of God will be your best weapon in your season of defense but also in the times when you display a strategic attack. When you seem to be pounded mercilessly by life, the Word of God will be an effective weapon in your defense. God's Word will equip you to stave off and even repel your attacker. When you regain your balance, the Word of God becomes your unparalleled weapon in your season of counter-attack. The devil has no recourse but to flee and attempt to fight another day.

Before we discuss how Victory Action 8: Live in the Word of God is immensely vital to your defensive and offensive strategies, we must first consider the why. Why does living in the Word of God take such a prominent place in standing firm against our spiritual enemies and in our personal rebuilding? I will suggest four reasons why living in the Word of God is tactically sound as you stand firm.

FIRST, THE BIBLE IS THE WORD OF GOD AND IT IS LIKE NO OTHER BOOK.

It is a manual instructing you on the meaning of life, the purpose of life, how to live life, and what happens to you after your life on earth is over. There is no other book written in history that contains the Truth, the power, and the life-transforming content found in the Bible. This is the source of all sources.

SECOND, THE BIBLE REVEALS WHO GOD IS.

When you read the Bible, you discover the character of God, how to know God, and how your relationship with God will change your life now and for eternity. If you want to know God, then you must read His book that He wrote for you! If you want God's help to get off the canvas of life and rebuild victoriously, then you must study who He is, learn what He wants you to do, and then obey His instructions.

THIRD, READING THE BIBLE BREATHES LIFE INTO YOUR SPIRIT.

"All Scripture is breathed out by God and is profitable for teaching, for reproof, for correction and for training in righteousness, that the man of God may be complete, equipped for every good work" (2 Timothy 3:16–17). All of God's Word is useful to you as it equips and empowers you to be like Him and to act like Him for His glory. When God breathed into man the breath of life, Adam became a living being (Genesis 2:7). In the same way, when you allow God-breathed Scripture into your heart and mind, you become alive in Him and experience life on a whole new level. Though your external circumstances may reek of destruction, if you live in the Word of God, you will experience internally the peace that surpasses all understanding, the joy of the Lord, and the hope of your salvation.

> If you want to know God, then you must read His book that He wrote for you! If you want God's help to get off the canvas of life and rebuild victoriously, then you must study who He is, learn what He wants you to do, and then obey His instructions.

FOURTH, THE WORD OF GOD IS GOD'S WORD TO YOU!

Yes, I mean you! Perhaps, you would like to talk with God on your cell phone now. While that is not possible, you can talk with Him anytime and that is called prayer. Also, you can delve into His Word and allow Scripture to speak to you! For example, as you read the Psalms, you can identify immediately with the writer as you feel his passion, ache with him in his dilemmas, and rejoice with him as he discovers the joy of being in God's presence. God's Word will come alive as you read it and it will resonate in your spirit because God is speaking to you specifically and directly from the pages in your Bible.

Now that we have considered why living in the Word of God is so important, we can use His Word to defend ourselves in life's daily spiritual battles. Living in the Word of God protects, equips, and empowers you to stand firm against your spiritual enemies and live victoriously in the midst of the most heated of battles. The reason is found in Hebrews 4:12, "For the word of God is living and active, sharper than any two-edged sword, piercing to division of soul and of spirit, of joints and of marrow, and discerns the thoughts and intentions of the heart."

God's Word is "living and active." As I mentioned, it is God-breathed which makes it a "living" document; it is just as genuine and relevant today as it was on the day it was written! God's Word does not have an expiration date, it does not lack the power to answer the problems of today, and it has not changed the definition of Truth in an effort to be more appealing to the masses.

God's Word is "sharper than any two-edged sword" as it penetrates and judges. The reason is God's Word is Truth, Light, Love, and

Life. When people encounter it, they are exposed for who they truly are. Their facades, pretenses, and accomplishments cannot withstand the comparison of who Truth declares who they should be.

When we are living in darkness and encounter light, we are exposed by that light for who we truly are. That light penetrates our self-made barriers and even our self-imposed rules for living. We are judged by the comparison and stand self-condemned because we choose the darkness rather than the light and do not meet the standard set by the light. Our situation is what it is and no amount of negotiating, pleading, whining, or even self-deprecating can change that fact.

With all of this in mind, you can stand firm against the attacks of your enemy with the sword of the Spirit as a defensive weapon. The tactics of the enemy used against you include lies, rumors, fear, doubt, chaos, isolation, and temptations. But none of these are from God! God is not the author of anxiety and death, but of peace and life. When Jesus was tempted by the devil as recorded in Matthew 4:1–11, He responded to the temptations of the devil by quoting God's Word at every point. Three times the devil tempted and three times Jesus responded with "It is written." Living in God's Word empowered our Lord with Truth and Love to withstand the attacks of the enemy.

Jesus could have engaged the devil in a power struggle and displayed his superior strength and authority. But in doing so, He would have lowered himself to the level of his aggressor. Fighting by the devil's rules would have raised the devil to a level of authority and importance that he does not have because he is not the equal, in any way, to the Son of God. Instead, Jesus let the Word of God do His talking for Him!

As I remember being knocked down to the lowest point in my life, the time when it seemed that I had to struggle to even breathe and I had lost my energy to function properly in life,

I remember the attacks of the enemy. He told me that I was worthless. He told me that my trusting in God was useless because if God loved me then I would not have been knocked down to the canvas of life. He told me that there was no hope, no rescue coming, and that my current situation in life was my new "normal." Had I listened to his lies, I would have been utterly and completely destroyed.

Thankfully, I found strength in God's Word! I made the specific choice not to believe the "father of lies" but instead to live in the Word of God and believe the Giver of Life. When I did not have the emotional energy to pray, I delved into the Psalms and read aloud, line by line, the Truth of God's Word. Instead of focusing on the lies, I immersed myself in God—in His Truth, His Love, and His Grace. God's Word solidified in my heart and mind that He loved me, that I was a child of the King, that He would walk with me even through the valley of the shadow of death, and that He would rescue me to fulfill my destiny that He ordained.

In spite of my external circumstances, I chose to live in God's Word and follow Him. Even in the moments of having no energy, I forced myself to be in the presence of people who loved the Lord and who would speak life into my heart. I was blessed that I could talk weekly with a pastor who used God's Word to counsel me. I purposed to apply to my life Victory Action 8: Live in God's Word and use the sword of the Spirit as a defensive weapon to stand firm against the enemy. And by the grace of God, I have seen the Lord rebuild my life and honor me by allowing me to serve Him as my life occupation.

Living in God's Word equips us to use the Bible as an offensive weapon, as well, and can be used in the heat of the most intense and life-threatening battles. God's Word equips you to win the day in your spiritual battles in the following actions.

FIRST, WHEN YOU LIVE IN GOD'S WORD, YOU ARE APPEALING TO THE HIGHEST AUTHORITY.

As highly as you might think of yourself, your chances of withstanding the temptations and spiritual attacks of the enemy alone are not very good; in fact, your defeat is guaranteed. Sorry to bring you the bad news, but you are incapable of defeating the devil on your own because he has a greater spiritual authority than you at this time. The apostle Paul taught us, "for all have sinned and fall short of the glory of God" (Romans 3:23). This is why we need a Savior!

When doubt, fear, anxiety, uncertainty, and anger rear their ugly heads and you are tempted to respond in ways that originate in your old nature, you can find victory for today by appealing to God's Word; the highest authority. There are times in your journey when the best response to being knocked down by life is to read God's Word and declare your belief in Him and His promises. When you draw the proverbial line in the sand and declare that you will stand on the Truth of God's Word then you are appealing to the highest authority. John gave us the reason when he wrote, "Little children, you are from God and have overcome them, for he who is in you is greater than he who is in the world" (1 John 4:4). Jesus is greater than the one who is in the world: the devil. All the devil can do is flee.

There is none greater than Jesus Christ. He is "I AM" (Exodus 3:14). He was and is and is to come (Revelation 4:8). God, "cannot be tempted with evil, and he himself tempts no one" (James 1:13). Romans 8:31 teaches us, "What then shall we say to these things? If God is for us, who can be against us?" When you read your Bible with an open heart ready to receive and obey, then you appeal to the highest authority.

SECOND, WHEN YOU LIVE IN GOD'S WORD YOU LIVE IN TRUTH.

Truth exposes the lies of the devil, just as the light reveals all things hidden previously in darkness. Already in this chapter, we quoted Hebrews 4:12 and it applies here as well, "For the word of God is living and active, sharper than any two-edged sword, piercing to the division of soul and of spirit, of joints and of marrow; and discerns the thoughts and intentions of the heart."

Remember that the devil is the author of lies. He will do everything he can to cause you to doubt, to fear, to feel guilty, to feel anxious, and to live a defeated life. But these feelings and thoughts are not from the Lord! God's Word teaches that you are "fearfully and wonderfully made" by God (Psalm 139:14) and that God loves you! He loves you so much that He gave His only Son to die in your place so that you can have eternal life (John 3:16)!

> Here's what you can do in your moments of doubt or fear. Take those feelings and thoughts and compare them to the Truth of God's Word. You will discover the truth that you are loved by God, that God is on your side, and that you will find victory as you remain faithful during your season of struggle. That is a guarantee!

Here's what you can do in your moments of doubt or fear. Take those feelings and thoughts and compare them to the Truth of God's Word. You will discover the truth that you are loved by God, that God is on your side, and that you will find victory as you remain faithful during your season of struggle. That is a guarantee!

THIRD, WHEN YOU LIVE IN GOD'S WORD, YOU ARE EQUIPPED TO RESPOND RIGHTEOUSLY.

The temptation you face is to respond in a manner that reflects how you were hurt. In fact, our sinful nature tells us to seek revenge, and if someone hurts you, then you are justified to hurt them more. But by taking this low road, you are fighting by the devil's rules. Instead, we can take the high road to freedom and victory by learning from God's Word how to respond righteously.

Previously, we considered how Jesus responded to the devil's temptation. He did not try to impress the enemy or overpower him. Instead, at every temptation, Jesus quoted God's Word in response. By living in the Word of God, Jesus was equipped to respond righteously.

In the Sermon on the Mount, Jesus taught us to love our enemies, to pray for those who persecute us, to avoid judging others, and to let the light of God's love shine through us. The Bible will provide instruction as to how you can respond to life's struggles. Search God's Word and be willing to obey what you are taught. In doing so, you will respond righteously. You will live without regrets and you will live in victory.

FOURTH, WHEN YOU LIVE IN GOD'S WORD YOU DISCOVER THAT YOUR WEAKNESSES ARE TURNED INTO STRENGTHS.

As you engage our spiritual enemy, you are not defined by your weaknesses but instead live as a member of the family of God and with the empowerment of the Holy Spirit of God. Let's look at the anger you feel that resulted from your being knocked to the canvas of life. Your old nature is screaming at you to get revenge, extract your pound of flesh, and even the score. You think that you may not totally recuperate your losses, but you will stand up for your rights! You know this line of thought because you have heard it from the voices in your head. But in your heart, you know such an approach is a reaction from your hurt and pain. This is not what God's Word instructs you to do. God wants to define your new reality by His Word.

Instead of focusing on your weaknesses, turn to God's Word, stand firm in His authority, and find strength! Here are some Bible verses that address a righteous response to anger, a response that will rebuild your life and bring victory!

- "Fret not yourself because of evildoers; be not envious of wrongdoers! For they will soon fade like the grass and wither, like the green herb. . . . Refrain from anger, and forsake wrath. Fret not yourself; it tends only to evil" (Psalms 37:1–2, 8).
- "Be anger do not sin: do not let the sun go down on your anger, and give no opportunity to the devil" (Ephesians 4:26–27).
- "'But I say to you, Do not resist the one who is evil. But if anyone slaps you on the right cheek, turn to him the other also'" (Matthew 5:39).
- "You have heard that it was said, 'You shall love your neighbor and hate your enemy.' But I say to you, love your enemies and pray for those who persecute you'" (Matthew 5:43–44).
- "Then Peter came up and asked, 'Lord, how often will my brother sin against me, and I forgive him? As many as seven times?' Jesus said to him, 'I do not say to you seven times, but seventy-seven times'" (Matthew 18:21–22).
- "Beloved, never avenge yourselves, but leave it to the wrath of God, for it is written, 'Vengeance is mine, I will repay,

says the Lord' To the contrary, 'if your enemy is hungry, feed him; if he is thirsty, give him something to drink; for by so doing you will heap burning coals on his head.'" (Romans 12:19–21).

When you address Victory Action 8: Live in the Word of God by filling your heart and mind with the Truth of God's Word then you are equipped to stand firm against the enemy defensively and offensively. Read God's Word daily! Read each verse of the Bible aloud and as a personal prayer. Apply these truths to your life every single day and in every single moment. Remember that:

- Knowing God's Word helps you to understand God's character.
- Living God's Word helps you to understand God's love.
- Sharing God's Word helps you to understand God's heart.

I end this chapter with Psalm 19:7–14:

> 7 *The law of the* Lord *is perfect,*
> *reviving the soul;*
> *the testimony of the* Lord *is sure,*
> *making wise the simple;*
> 8 *the precepts of the* Lord *are right,*
> *rejoicing the heart;*
> *The commandment of the* Lord *is pure,*
> *enlightening the eyes;*
> 9 *the fear of the* Lord *is clean,*
> *enduring forever;*
> *the rules of the* Lord *are true,*
> *and righteous altogether.*

¹⁰ *More desired are they than gold,*
even much pure gold;
sweeter also than honey
and drippings from the honeycomb.
¹¹ *Moreover by them is your servant is warned;*
in keeping them there is great reward.
¹² *Who can discern his errors?*
Declare me innocent from hidden faults.
¹³ *Keep back your servant also from presumptuous sins;*
let them not have dominion over me!
Then I shall be blameless,
And innocent of great transgression.
¹⁴ *Let the words of my mouth and*
this meditation of my heart
be acceptable in your sight,
O LORD, my rock and my redeemer.

FOR YOU TO CONSIDER

1. Compile reasons why you must apply the Word of God, the Bible, to your daily life.

2. There were four actions given to you that reveal how God's Word equips you to win your spiritual battles. Share how each of them are relevant to your life and what your response will be.

3. Read Psalm 19:7–14 and write what the Lord is saying to you.

SCRIPTURE FOR YOU TO PRAY TODAY

"Everyone then who hears these words of mine and does them will be like a wise man who built his house on the rock" (Matthew 7:24).

What is the Lord saying to you right now?

VICTORY ACTION 9

PRAY IN THE SPIRIT

ALIGN YOURSELF WITH THE HOLY SPIRIT

"Praying at all times in the Spirit, with all prayer and supplication."

EPHESIANS 6:18A

"Not by might, nor by power, but by my Spirit,' says the LORD of hosts."

ZECHARIAH 4:6

The missionary stood at the fork of the road deep in the bush of Tanzania. In front of him sat a man who held the information that could save the life of the grandma in his vehicle. Just a few minutes before, the woman was sitting at the edge of tall, thick brush but with her feet stretched out in the dirt path. A vehicle drove by and caught her by such surprise that it ran over her leg and left her foot dangling from her tibia.

The missionary, who was driving the vehicle behind the accident, stopped immediately and sought to provide aid. The woman went into shock instantly. Instinctively, she attempted to put her foot back in place and applied mud to her injury as if to glue her body back together. The missionary knew that her life was in jeopardy and she needed to be in a hospital immediately. But they were in the heart of the country and finding medical attention in time would require a miracle. So he responded by doing what he had be trained to do; he prayed and asked the Holy Spirit to give him wisdom.

Suddenly, the woman's grandson appeared, as if out of nowhere. While the missionary spoke Swahili, he did not speak the local dialect of the grandma. But the grandson spoke both and so served as the interpreter. The grandson heard that there was a hospital, but he did not know exactly where it was. While the two vehicles went north, the missionary prayed that they would find someone who could provide directions.

This led them to the fork in the road. At this point you had a fifty-fifty chance of guessing correctly, but the wrong road would lead them kilometers out of the way, and the grandma would bleed to death. The vehicles stopped and the missionary prayed. Then, he noticed a man seated by the side of the road on the right! In Swahili, he asked the man for directions to the hospital. Without hesitation, the man pointed to the road on his left. When the missionary took a step toward his vehicle, the Holy Spirit spoke to his heart and said, "That is not right! Ask the grandson to ask the man in their local dialect." The missionary did just that and had the grandson ask for directions. Immediately, the man pointed to the road on his right!

Believing now that they had the proper directions, the two vehicles took the road on their left and discovered within fifteen *minutes a hospital with a qualified medical team. The operation on the grandma began within the hour, and her foot and her life was saved.*

The beauty of Victory Action 9: Pray in the Spirit is that you do not overcome your trials and rebuild on your own. If only you ask, you can have the Holy Spirit of God, the third member of the Trinity, as your Counselor, Teacher, Guide, and Proclaimer of Truth in your life. He will give you strength to stand firm, equip you to thrive in a victorious lifestyle, and empower you to help others in their most difficult spiritual battles.

So throw off the mind-set that you are self-sufficient and that you can battle alone. That kind of thinking may have contributed to your personal drama and limits you to respond properly. Instead, ask the Lord to take control of your life in a deeper way. In Ephesians 6:18, he apostle Paul instructs us: "praying at all times in the Spirit, with all prayer and supplication." Paul gave us four directives in this verse.

FIRST, YOU ARE TO PRAY!

Talk to God and ask that His will be done in your life. In fact, Jesus told you to pray this very prayer in Matthew 6:9–13, "Pray then like this: 'Our Father in heaven, hallowed be your name. Your kingdom come, your will be done, on earth as it is in heaven. Give us this day our daily bread, and forgive us our debts, as we also have forgiven our debtors. And lead us not into temptation, but deliver us from the evil.'"

As we consider this briefly, we can highlight key elements of this prayer.

1. You are talking to Almighty God, the Creator of heaven and earth. There is none greater, stronger, or more faithful. He is the very definition of Love. He is so awesome that His name is, "I AM" (Exodus 3:14).

2. Every time you interact with God, you must give Him honor, and glory, and respect so you say hallowed (or "holy") is your name. You are the inferior being addressing your Superior with humility and respect.

3. We declare that we want His will to be done, and therefore, He is the Master and we are His servants.

4. You are then instructed to ask the Lord for His provision to bring the victory for your physical needs, for matters of your heart, and for victory over sin.

5. Repenting and receiving God's forgiveness is an amazing gift of freedom that clears your conscience and propels you forward to walk in victory.

Remember, God is also your Heavenly Father, and He will pour out His blessings on you abundantly to overflowing! So no matter if your personal drama just started or if you addressed your defensive deficiencies and are now advancing in your offensive strategy, going to God and asking for His will to be done in your life is the best move you can make.

SECOND, YOU ARE TO PRAY IN THE SPIRIT!

Paul's instruction is not to just pray, but to pray in the Spirit. This means that you ask to be filled with the Holy Spirit; heart, mind, and soul. When the Spirit dwells in our lives, we are empowered with the very presence of God. We will discuss this more below.

THIRD, YOU ARE TO PRAY IN THE SPIRIT ON ALL OCCASIONS!

Prayer should be your first response and not your last resort. Pray for wisdom, guidance, creativity, answers, help, advice, blessing, divine appointments to share your faith, opportunities to bless others, healing, daily provisions, future plans, your family, freedom from the chains of sin that so easily entangle you . . . and the list goes on.

Prayer should be your ongoing conversation with the Lord. Sure, you pray in church, but you need to also pray at home, in your car, at work, on the bus, at meal time, in the morning, in the afternoon, in the evening, when you first awake, and even before your nightly sleep. The Lord is your friend who wants—and deserves—to engage you at all times. Prayer keeps you aligned properly in your relationship with Him.

> So pray about everything! Pray all the time! You cannot rebuild your life on your own, nor should you use your own blueprint. Get God involved and follow His will, and you will be amazed at what He will do in your life.

SO PRAY ABOUT EVERYTHING! PRAY ALL THE TIME!

You cannot rebuild your life on your own, nor should you use your own blueprint. Get God involved and follow His will, and you will be amazed at what He will do in your life. Seek to glorify God the Father, to obey God the Son, and to be led and empowered by God the Holy Spirit.

Prayer is the means to a relationship with God that involves listening and speaking, acting and reacting. Victory Action 9: Pray in the Spirit means that we are in submission to God so that His

Holy Spirit can empower us for His glory. Your relationship with the Holy Spirit is just as vital to your spiritual growth and maturity as it was to the disciples in the first century. Jesus told His disciples to wait in Jerusalem until they were baptized by the Holy Spirit (Acts 1:4–5). He then said,

The vibrant relationship between the Holy Spirit and the first century believers is available for the taking for you today!

"But you will receive power when the Holy Spirit has come upon you, and you will be my witnesses in Jerusalem and in all Judea and Samaria, and to the ends of the earth" (Acts 1:8). In other words, do not go anywhere or do anything until you are first empowered by the Holy Spirit.

The disciples waited, as recorded in Acts 2, and the Holy Spirit was poured upon them individually in an amazing way. These believers were then empowered and emboldened to change their known world so effectively that this would resonant throughout history to this very day. As we read the book of Acts, we see how the Holy Spirit worked in the lives of believers. The Spirit was their Counselor and Comforter. He was the One who gave them clarity to see and hear the will of God. He gave them the strength and boldness to be obedient to God's calling and to stand boldly in proclamation before even the fiercest of foes. He brought to their memory the teachings of Christ so that they would stand firm in His spiritual authority. The vibrant relationship between the Holy Spirit and the first century believers is available for the taking for you today! I encourage you to read the Book of Acts in one sitting with the intent of observing how the Holy Spirit enabled and empowered the disciples to do God's will and for His glory.

Here is what you can do now. Ask the Holy Spirit to take control of your life completely; heart, mind, soul, and strength. The starting point is to pray Psalm 139:23–24, "Search me, O God, and know my heart! Try me and know my thoughts. And see if there be any grievous way in me, and lead me in the way everlasting." Open the entirety of your being, empty yourself of anything, small or large, that will hinder the move of God in your life, then allow the Spirit of God to fill you to overflowing. In fact, read all of Psalm 139, and you will gain a clearer understand of the meaning of those final two verses of this great chapter.

As you grow in your relationship with the Holy Spirit, you will discover new adventures with the Lord will open and your character will develop to be the person that He created you to be. The apostle Paul wrote about this in Galatians 5 as he taught us about living in the fullness and freedom of a relationship with Jesus Christ and the Holy Spirit. In the beginning portion of the chapter, he taught that Christ brings freedom from sin and spiritual bondage. The quality of our walk with Him is not determined by our ability to keep rules and regulations set by our religion but by love; "The only thing that counts is faith expressing itself through love" (Galatians 5:6, NIV). The power to live in love comes through a relationship with the Holy Spirit as seen in the last half of Galatians 5. Paul teaches that the sinful nature, our former self, is directly contrary to life in the Holy Spirit.

Open the entirety of your being, empty yourself of anything, small or large, that will hinder the move of God in your life, then allow the Spirit of God to fill you to overflowing.

Paul listed with the acts of the sinful nature: "sexual immorality, impurity, sensuality, idolatry, sorcery, enmity, strife, jealousy, fits of rage, rivalries, dissensions, divisions, envy, drunkenness, orgies, and things like these. I warn you, as I warned you before, that those who do such things will not inherit the kingdom of God" (Galatians 5:19–21). These self-centered, self-serving, and self-gratifying behaviors lead to spiritual death! Thank the Lord that we have been freed from this! We can throw off these acts, like filthy rags, and toss them in the rubbish bin. These are the very acts that led to our personal drama and our being knocked to the canvas of life in seeming defeat!

> **Genuine, life-changing, spiritual freedom comes when we purpose to change. We allow the Holy Spirit to take up residence in our heart, mind, and soul, and we ask Him to empower us to walk and talk and act and react like Jesus.**

Genuine, life-changing, spiritual freedom comes when we purpose to change. We allow the Holy Spirit to take up residence in our heart, mind, and soul, and we ask Him to empower us to walk and talk and act and react like Jesus. When we activate Victory Action 9: Pray in the Spirit in our lives daily, we will see what Paul calls, "the fruit of the Spirit" overflowing from us and onto everyone we encounter and in every situation of life.

> *"But the fruit of the Spirit is love, joy, peace, patience, kindness, goodness, faithfulness, gentleness, and self-control; against such things there is no law. And those who belong to Christ Jesus have crucified the flesh with its passions and desires. If we live by the Spirit, let us also keep in step with the Spirit. Let us not become conceited, provoking one another, envying one other"* (Galatians 5:22–26).

So once you receive freedom from the ways of our old nature, the flesh, you can replace them with the fruit of the Spirit. Each day, and at each encounter, you can pause and ask, "What should be my loving response?" You can learn to live in the joy and peace of the Lord. In fact, Romans 15:13 tells us, "May the God of hope fill you with all joy and peace in believing, so that by the power of the Holy Spirit you may abound in hope." Learning to trust the Lord reaps a personal harvest of hope, joy, and peace. I encourage you to consider each aspect of the fruit of the Spirit and seek Him to make it part in your daily routine. At first, it may seem awkward, but after a time it will become so natural that the fruit of the Spirit will be embedded into your character!

I remind you that the power you need to fulfill the Victory Actions we have discussed does not come from within you or from anything that you can manufacture. The power you need to be the person God created you to be comes from an intimate and daily relationship with the Holy Spirit. Like it says in Zechariah 4:6, "'Not by might, nor by power, but by my Spirit,' says the Lord of hosts."

As you move forward to live in the fullness of a follower of Jesus Christ, you can stand firm against temptation knowing that you have "crucified the flesh with its passions and desires" (Galatians 5:24). You can go beyond saying no to our spiritual enemy by responding in a way that solidifies your faith in God by living in the Spirit and keeping "in step with the Spirit" (Galatians 5: 25). The spiritual goal that we each strive for is to be like Christ. As we do, we are empowered by the Holy Spirit to embrace His thoughts as our thoughts, His teaching as our way of life, and His will to be the desired fulfillment of our heart.

Whether we are rebuilding our lives or facing our spiritual enemy one more time, we must seek to activate each of the Victory

Actions as we are led, empowered, and encouraged by the Holy Spirit. He will give us to strength and ability to put on the whole armor of God and to stand firm in truth, righteousness, peace, faith, hope, and the Word of God. All we need do is be spiritually astute and pray "at all times in the Spirit, with all prayer and supplication."

It will be in your best interest to set and keep an appointment with the Holy Spirit each day. Hopefully, you have already set a time when you separate yourself from the noise of life and get time—quality time—alone with God. Inviting the Holy Spirit of God to recalibrate your motives and thoughts, and evaluate your life honestly, will realign your life properly and situate you in a position of victory. As you embrace God's Word in daily readings, ask the Holy Spirit to enlighten you to the meaning of what you read as well as to empower you to apply the Truth of God's Word to your life daily. As you reframe your conversations and meetings of the previous day, ask the Holy Spirit to give you understanding and wisdom. As you consider the upcoming events of the day and week, ask the Holy Spirit to guide you to do that which will bring glory to God.

> **Whether we are rebuilding our lives or facing our spiritual enemy one more time, we must seek to activate each of the Victory Actions as we are led, empowered, and encouraged by the Holy Spirit.**

You must not neglect Victory Action 9: Pray in the Spirit. Trying to thrive in a life of victory without praying in the Spirit will be as successful as entering Monaco Grand Prix with a race car that does not have an engine. It just does not make sense! Also, neglecting to pray in the Spirit is exactly what your enemy, the devil, wants you to do. Your unwillingness to address this spiritual discipline gives him a foothold, an open door, into your heart. Since he cannot impede you from praying in the Spirit, his only hope is that your spiritual decline is self-inflicted. He will do his best to tempt you, discourage you, and mock you. But the only one who can stop you from developing your relationship with the Lord is you.

> **Take time daily to invest in your relationship with the Holy Spirit. Allow Him to lead, empower, and equip you to fulfill all that Christ has commanded, so you can glorify God with your life.**

The response to this Victory Action is found in the Galatians 5:22–26 passage and specifically Galatians 5:25, "If we live by the Spirit, let us keep in step with the Spirit." Take time daily to invest in your relationship with the Holy Spirit. Allow Him to lead, empower, and equip you to fulfill all that Christ has commanded, so you can glorify God with your life. This is a key step as you continue your upward and onward march to victory and "pray in the Spirit on all occasions with all kinds of prayers and requests" (Ephesians 6:18, NIV). This is the tested and true action of champions!

FOR YOU TO CONSIDER

1. What changes must you make to pray regularly each day?

2. Create your prayer list that you can use daily.

3. Ask the Lord to assist you in praying in the Spirit.

4. Consider each item listed in the "fruit of the Spirit" in Galatians 5:22–26, and state what you must do to activate them in your life.

SCRIPTURE FOR YOU TO PRAY TODAY

"But the fruit of the Spirit is love, joy, peace, patience, kindness, goodness, faithfulness, gentleness and self-control; against such things there is no law. And those who belong to Christ Jesus have crucified the flesh with its passions and desires. If we live by the Spirit, let us keep in step with the Spirit. Let us not become conceited, provoking one another, envying one other" (Galatians 5:22–26).

What is the Lord saying to you right now?

VICTORY ACTION 10

BE ALERT AND
PRAY FOR GOD'S PEOPLE
BE A BLESSING TO OTHERS

*"To that end, keep alert with all perseverance,
making supplication for all the saints."*

EPHESIANS 6:18B

*"Of Issachar, men who had understanding of the
times, to know what Israel ought to do."*

1 CHRONICLES 12:32

The soldier fought gallantly that day on the muddy and blood-stained battlefield. The hated enemy pressed forward but he was standing firm with his battalion to declare, "No more! Your advance ends today!" But his ability to thwart the enemy came to an immediate halt when he *was dropped to his knees by a sniper's bullet that shattered his right forearm.*

Within minutes, the medics found him and were carrying him off the battlefield. But the soldier stopped them and pointed to a fellow warrior who needed medical assistance more than he. Knowing that bleeding out was a distinct possibility, he knew that he could not live with himself if his colleague died.

Instead of turning away from the heat of battle, the soldier found other wounded whose bodies scattered across the meadow, abandoned and screaming for help. He discovered an inner strength to carry fellow warriors off the battlefield to safety. Not satisfied with saving one life, he reentered the field of battle. He continued this process until the sun descended past the horizon. Exhausted, he relented that he did all that his strength allowed. Dozens upon dozens of men were saved that day and made it home to tell their wives and children of the one who risked his life on their behalf.

One man, who placed the lives of his fellow brothers over his own, did what was needed to be done. While he would continue to fight the internal guilt of not being able to save every wounded soldier, the families of those he did save thanked the good Lord for his bravery and for bringing home their loved ones.

We have made it to the final victory action! Victory Action 10 is Be Alert and Pray for God's People. This comes from Ephesians 6:18b which reads, "To that end, keep alert with all perseverance, making supplication for all the saints." Let us consider the phrases in this verse.

FIRST, "TO THAT END" DIRECTS YOU TO BE MINDFUL OF OUR ENTIRE STUDY UP TO THIS POINT.

You were knocked down by life. You considered with me the defensive strategy so you would not be hit again. Then, we studied Ephesians 6 to learn how life could be rebuilt as the core of an offensive strategy which leads to a victorious life. Now, we see Paul admonishing you to remember all that you were taught; "to that end." Learn your lessons. Apply God's truth to your life. Work diligently to rebuild your life as you are led by the principles of the Bible and specifically the passages discussed in our study. Choose life. Discover freedom that comes only by serving the Lord and living by His rules.

Choose life. Discover freedom that comes only by serving the Lord and living by His rules.

SECOND, "KEEP ALERT" DIRECTS YOU TO BE LIKE THE MIGHTY MEN OF ISSACHAR.

They "had understanding of the times, to know what Israel ought to do" (1 Chronicles 12:32).

Stay awake spiritually. Be vigilant to keep guard of yourself personally, your family, and those in your circle of influence. Be aware of where you are in your walk with the Lord, set goals for growth, and create strategies to achieve those goals.

Also, being alert is a challenge to choose how you will respond when life takes another punch at you. It is your choice to keep focused on Jesus in spite of the circumstances. For example, in Philippians 4, the apostle Paul wrote, "I have learned in whatever situation I am in to be content. I know how to be brought low, and I know how to abound. In any and every circumstance, I have learned the secret of facing plenty and hunger, abundance and need. *I can do all things through him who gives me strength*" (Philippians 4:11–13, emphasis added).

Again, I remind you of Habakkuk 3:17–19, "Though the fig tree should not blossom, nor fruit be on the vines, the produce of the olive fail and the fields yield no food, the flock be cut off from the fold and there be no herd in the stalls, *yet I will rejoice in the LORD; I will be take joy in the God of my salvation.* GOD, the Lord, is my strength; he makes my feet like the deer's; he makes me tread on my high places" (emphasis added).

Even when life knocks you down to the point of physical suffering, you will find strength in the response of believers who endured the harshest persecution. In Acts 5:41 we read, "[The apostles] left the presence of the council, rejoicing that they were counted worthy to suffer dishonor for the name."

Choose to be content, to rejoice, and to consider it an honor to suffer for the Name of Jesus. You can control your thoughts. When challenged, you can find encouragement from God's Word and also from other believers who will stand with you in support.

Being alert is a positive challenge, as well, because you have a choice as to how you will live. You can choose to honor God in your time at work, time at leisure, time with loved ones, time with people who cannot repay you readily, and even how you spend your money. It is your choice!

Being alert equips you to take control of your life and positions you to receive benefits. The benefits that come your way will include living a life without regret, living a life "of power, and of love, and of a sound mind" (2 Timothy 1:7, KJV), and living a life that establishes your legacy. It is a life that will make your children proud and want to emulate you. Most importantly, being alert with the truths of God's Word will align you with the Will of God and help you grow in obedience to Him in your life journey.

Our study together brings a defensive and offensive strategy as to how you will respond to the events of life that bring anxiety, fear, bewilderment, and a sense of hopelessness. You can put on the whole armor of God and stand firm. You can live in truth, righteousness, peace, faith, hope, with the Word of God, and pray in the Spirit. You are equipped for the fight! God is on your side and the Holy Spirit is present to counsel and empower you to victory. You are not alone as you have a community of Christian brothers and sisters in Christ who will support and encourage you during your life challenge. You are an overcomer!

> You can put on the whole armor of God and stand firm. You can live in truth, righteousness, peace, faith, hope, with the Word of God, and pray in the Spirit. You are equipped to fight! God is on your side and the Holy Spirit is present to counsel and empower you to victory.

THIRD, "ALWAYS KEEP ON PRAYING FOR ALL THE LORD'S PEOPLE" (NIV).

The last part of Ephesians 6:18 is a directive that challenges you to live beyond being self-focused to thrive in Christian community where you encourage and edify others.

Life's trials can knock us out of balance and make us so self-focused that we lose sight of God's call on our lives and the fact we are blessed to be a blessing to others. A natural response to being knocked down by life is self-protection and withdrawing from life for self-examination. This is appropriate, but only for a season. We need times to pull back from life, so that we can evaluate, heal, and be energized. But times of being self-focused must be defined clearly or we will disqualify ourselves from living life as God intended.

An indicator of where you are in the process of rebuilding your life is how engaged with others you can be without drawing attention to yourself or rehashing the dramas of your life, or if you are avoiding relationships to live in isolation. Caring for others—genuinely caring for others—is a positive indicator that healing is occurring and you are on the road to victory. Healthy people can rely on the Lord to deal with their life issues and to bless others.

> **Caring for others—genuinely caring for others—is a positive indicator that healing is occurring and you are on the road to victory. Healthy people can rely on the Lord to deal with their life issues and to bless others.**

Life has meaning when we live in God's context. He did not create you to live alone but to be engaged with others. While you may, or may not, be blessed by being with everyone you encounter in your daily life, you can be a blessing and a positive influence to them. When you are living in God's context, you are engaged actively with family, friends, the Christian community, and those who are in the world. True living does not focus on me, my wants, my desires, or my cravings, but on how together we can fulfill God's will in our lives. The concept of living life to the fullest finds fulfillment as we are connected with others in righteous relationships. A life focused on self is just that: a selfish life that loves things and uses people instead of loving people and using things.

Paul was teaching you to "keep on praying for all the Lord's people" (NIV). Our response to this begins by following the directive: pray! We pray for each other for all aspects of life such as protection, healing, victory over sin, rescue from temptation, and direction from God. The list is seemingly endless because we are to pray about everything! Prayer unites us with those for whom we are praying and it unites us with the Lord. Prayer helps us understand better the situations of the ones needing prayer and challenges us to go beyond a superficial response. In fact, when we take seriously our responsibility to pray, we will discover that this leads us to move into tangible action when given opportunity.

The Bible has so many verses that encourage you to be a blessing to others. Here are some for you to consider:

- "Whoever brings blessing will be enriched, and one who waters will himself be watered" (Proverbs 11:25).
- "Whoever is generous to the poor lends to the Lord, and he will repay him for his deed" (Proverbs 19:17).
- "A generous man will himself be blessed" (Proverbs 22:9a, NIV).
- "The point is this: Whoever sows sparingly will also reap sparingly, and whoever sows bountifully will also reap bountifully. Each one must give what he has decided in his heart, not reluctantly or under compulsion, for God loves a cheerful giver. And God is able to make all grace abound to you, so that having all sufficiency in all things at all times, you will abound in every good work" (2 Corinthians 9:6–8).
- "Religion that is pure and undefiled before God the Father is this: to visit orphans and widows in their affliction, and to keep oneself unstained from the world" (James 1:27).
- "What good is it, my brothers, if someone says he has faith but does not have works? Can that faith save him? If a brother or sister is poorly clothed and lacking in daily food, and one of you says to them, "Go in peace, be warmed and filled," without giving them the things needed for the body,

what good is that? So also faith by itself, if it does not have works, is dead" (James 2:14–17).

- "Bear one other's burdens, and so fulfill the law of Christ" (Galatians 6:2).

When you care for other people you will receive the reward of feeling good about your actions because helping others is the right action to do. But the Lord also sees what you do and will reward you accordingly because He blesses those who bless others.

It should be noted that Paul exhorts you to pray continually "for all the saints." You are in a community of believers who form the family of God; they are your brothers and sisters. Your bond with them is not made because you have the same economic status or ethnicity, or even because you are friends. Your bond is forged by the blood of Jesus, which is a way of saying that your acceptance into the family of God is due solely to your obedience in following Jesus Christ.

Just as you are to take care of your personal family, as seen in 1 Timothy 5:8, you are to take care of those in the family of God. In Acts 2, we read of people who were Christ-followers and then baptized by the Holy Spirit (verse 4). The apostle Peter stood before a crowd, preached a sermon and "Those who received his word were baptized, and there were added that day about three thousand souls" (Acts 2:41). What follows immediately in this chapter is an account of how these new believers interacted with each other.

They considered themselves to be members of this new community, devoted to the apostles' teaching and to fellowship with other believers. Verse 44 reads, "All who believed were together and had all things in common." The results were that they enjoyed "favor with all the people. And the Lord added to their number day by day those who were being saved" (Acts 2:47). Taking care of each other in their community was a practice application of John 13:35: "By this all people will know that you are my disciples, if you have love for one another." The believers care for each other was a testimony to unbelievers of the love of Jesus Christ. So your priority as you seek to grow in your relationship with Jesus is to "Love the Lord your God with all your heart and with all your soul and with all your mind. This is the great and first commandment. And the second is like it: "You shall love your neighbor as yourself"" (Matthew 22:37–39). Your "neighbor" is first, but not limited to, your brothers and sisters in Christ.

We are not to neglect the poor, nor are we to overlook our responsibility to reach unbelievers with the love of Christ. We can do both. But your blessing of others can start within the community of faith and continue in outreach to those in the world.

Victory Action 10: Be Alert and Pray for God's People is vital to your spiritual health and well-being. Life knocked you down. But when you stand, regain your balance, and follow diligently after God, you will discover that you will bring others with you. In a sense, you have multiplied yourself as you stand with others. Instead of being in the boxing ring of life by yourself with the devil, you stand with the family of God. You are not alone.

> Life knocked you down. But when you stand, regain your balance, and follow diligently after God, you will discover that you will bring others with you. In a sense, you have multiplied yourself as you stand with others. . . . You are not alone.

Be like the man who was knocked to the canvas of life. He focused on Christ, took control of his personal drama, and rebuilt his life by the principles of God's Word. In this process, he invested in his three children so that they would be equipped to engage in the battles of life. His attitude was, "You may have knocked me down, but I will do my best to ensure that the three who follow me are victorious." While they have to fight their own battles, and engage the enemy in their own seasons of life, they would enter the ring knowing the One who stands with them and for them and His name is Jesus.

FOR YOU TO CONSIDER

1. Share about how the admonition to "be alert" applies to your life and what you must do in response.

2. Name five specific people and/or situations and pray for them.

3. How can you tangibly be a blessing to others? Select three people who need someone to bless them and ask the Lord what you can do in response.

SCRIPTURE FOR YOU TO PRAY TODAY

"Carry each other's burdens, and in this way you will fulfill the law of Christ" (Galatians 6:2).

What is the Lord saying to you right now?

CONCLUSION

CHOOSE LIFE!

L et me tell you something you already know. *The world ain't all sunshine and rainbows. It's a very mean and nasty place, and I don't care how tough you are, it will beat you to your knees and keep you there permanently if you let it. You, me, or nobody is gonna hit as hard as life. But it ain't about how hard you hit. It's about how hard you can get hit and keep moving forward; how much you can take and keep moving forward. That's how winning is done! Now, if you know what you're worth, then go out and get what you're worth. But you gotta be willing to take the hits, and not pointing fingers saying you ain't where you wanna be because of him or her or anybody. Cowards do that and that ain't you. You're better than that! I'm always gonna love you, no matter what. No matter what happens. You're my son and you're my blood. You're the best thing in my life. But until you start believing in yourself, you ain't gonna have a life."*

—Rocky Balboa to his son in *Rocky Balboa*[1]

---

1 *Rocky Balboa*, directed by Sylvester Stallone. Culver City, CA: Metro-Goldwyn-Mayer Studios Inc., 2006.

When life knocked me down I was told with kindness and grace by an amazing Christian couple that the Lord would see me through the trial and that there will be better days ahead. Though it was impossible for me to see anything good while I was tasting the canvas after my knockdown, I took them at their word. They had experienced a similar trial. They stood firm in their walk with the Lord and He empowered them to rebuild their lives. They were, and are, a success story!

So be encouraged! No matter where you are in your personal drama that knocked you down, I want to encourage you to stand firm. God is with you and better days are ahead! I can say this because throughout history that were others who endured your same trial and yet stood firm in the Lord. God is faithful and "is the same yesterday, today, and forever" (Hebrews 13:8). He is faithful to you, as well!

God is with you and better days are ahead!

As the title of this book is, *Stand Firm: What to Do When Life Knocks You Down*, it seems right to provide a biblical testimony of one who survived being knocked down by the grace of God and whose life was rebuilt to serve a greater purpose. I leave you with an example from the Old Testament, the story of a man named Joseph. You can relate to his personal drama on some level. Be encouraged that, like Joseph, God is on your side, He will never leave you or forsake you, and He will rebuild your life, for His glory.

Here are some events of the life of Joseph:

- Joseph was born into the family of Jacob who was the son of Isaac and the grandson of Abraham. Joseph was the eleventh son of twelve sons. Spending most of his childhood as the youngest of eleven sons could not have been an easy life for Joseph.

- When Joseph was seventeen years old, "his brothers saw that their father loved him more than all his brothers, they hated him and could not speak peacefully to him" (Genesis 37:4). The actions of his brothers had to have been very hurtful to Joseph, especially when he did nothing to deserve their hatred.

- Then God gave Joseph a dream. He told his brothers his dream and they "hated him even more" (Genesis 37:5). Joseph complicated his relationship with his brothers when he revealed this dream. This did not endear him to them in the slightest.

- "His brothers were jealous of him, but his father kept the saying in mind" (Genesis 37:11). The passage does not mention how their jealousy was revealed in daily life, but it had to have impacted Joseph negatively. No doubt, they belittled him at every opportunity and did whatever they could to make his life miserable.

- His brothers "conspired against him to kill him" (Genesis 37:18). How crushing it must have been for Joseph to learn that his brothers actually plotted to kill him! This goes against everything they believed and valued. This was a devastating nightmare from which one seemingly could not return.

- Reuben suggested a plan to throw Joseph into a cistern instead of killing him (Genesis 37:21–22). Reuben's intent was to get Joseph out of sight so his brothers would calm down, then rescue him and return him home safely. One wonders what is going through Joseph's mind while trapped in a dry cistern. Did he know Reuben's plan? Did he take seriously his brothers' plan and think that he was going to die? Did he cry out to his brothers to end this nightmare and get him home? Did he call out to God? He must have felt rejected, scared, and alone. The very ones who were supposed to protect him had turned against him.

- His brothers sold Joseph into slavery for twenty shekels of silver to Ishmaelites who took him to Egypt (Genesis 37:28). Rather than kill Joseph, Judah saw an opportunity to get rid of him by selling him.

> **[Joseph] used his faith as a strength, a way to survive being knocked to the canvas of life, and rebuilt his life based on his new circumstances.**

While the brothers lived with the consequences of selling their brother into slavery, they tried to appease their guilt by reasoning that at least they did not kill him. Joseph's nightmare went from bad to worse as he was sold into slavery and taken to a foreign land. Rejected, threatened, and sold into slavery. I wonder if he cried out, "God, where are you?" His life was altered forever as he was forced into an alternative reality created by the sins of his brothers.

- The Midianites sold Joseph to Potiphar, one of Pharaoh's officials, the captain of the guard (Genesis 37:36).
- Joseph was in a pagan land and was isolated and alone (Genesis 39:1). Rejected, abandoned, and forgotten by his loved ones, Joseph could have gone into a deep depression and turned away from his faith. Instead, he used his faith as a strength, a way to survive being knocked to the canvas of life, and rebuilt his life based on his new circumstances. The result was that "the LORD was with Joseph, and he became a successful man" (Genesis 39:2). Instead of blaming God, Joseph stood firm in his faith in Him and this resulted in

everyone around Joseph being blessed. In fact, Joseph honored God, in spite of his environment, and this led to Potiphar placing him in charge of his entire household. And he thrived as God's blessing was on them.

- Then, Joseph was falsely accused of sexual assault by Potiphar's wife and thrown into prison (Genesis 37:6–20). Just as life had turned the corner for good, someone betrayed him and knocked him onto the canvas one more time. Though he was falsely accused and completely innocent of the charges, Joseph was thrown into prison. I find it interesting that while Potiphar "burned with anger" (Genesis 37:19), he did not kill Joseph, but instead had him imprisoned. No doubt Joseph cried out, "God, what is going on here?" Betrayed . . . again! Rejected . . . again! Alone . . . again! If anyone had the right to think God had abandoned him, it was Joseph. Instead, he must have known that his imprisonment was not due to God's actions but the sinfulness of others. So Joseph stood firm.

- Once again, Joseph won favor with God and "the keeper of the prison put Joseph in charge of all the prisoners who were in the prison" (Genesis 39:22). Life kept knocking down Joseph, but Joseph kept getting back to his feet! But how? "The LORD was with Joseph and showed him steadfast love and gave him favor in the sight of the keeper of the prison" (Genesis 37:21). Once again, instead of quitting on God, Joseph allowed his faith in God to never wavered and he prospered.

- Two men in the prison—the cupbearer and the baker—had dreams, and Joseph interpreted their dreams. He told the cupbearer, "Only remember me, when it is well with you, and please do me the kindness to mention me to Pharaoh, and so get me out of this house" (Genesis 40:14). The cupbearer was restored; however, he "did not remember Joseph, but forgot him" (Genesis 40:23). Even though life was bearable in prison, Joseph was still in prison. He used his God-given gift for interpreting dreams to give him hope of one day being released. But once again, he was forgotten by someone who should have helped him. I wonder what Joseph was thinking when he realized that the cupbearer had failed him. Did he feel betrayed again? Rejected again? And alone . . . again? Did he wonder, "God, why does this keep happening to me?"

- Two years later, Pharaoh has two dreams that no one in Egypt could interpret. The cupbearer then remembered Joseph and brought him before Pharaoh. Two years had passed with no hint of rescue. Suddenly, Joseph was called before the mightiest man in the known world with the challenge of a lifetime: interpret Pharaoh's dream. Joseph interpreted the dream and was rewarded by being promoted to being second in all the land: only Pharaoh himself was higher (Genesis 41). I believe that Joseph kept faith in God during these two years because when called upon to interpret, he was ready to respond. This tells me that he was still in relationship with the Lord, and Joseph did not allow himself to quit on life. It is interesting that his reward was not his release. Instead, God's plan was in full action. Joseph was there for a purpose, one that no one could have anticipated. His journey from the bottom of the cistern in his homeland as a young person to now being a man at age 30 and serving Pharaoh had amazing turns, knockdowns, and discouragements. But Joseph kept battling, kept getting back on his feet, and never, ever quit. During the journey his was unaware that God was orchestrating the events of his life to fulfill His will for His people.

- Seven years later, the famine that Pharaoh's dreams had fore-told hit all of the known world. Jacob, Joseph's father, sent his sons to Egypt to find grain (Genesis 42:1–2). When they arrived, they soon found themselves bowing down to "the governor of the land. He was the one who sold grain to all the people of the land" (Genesis 42:6). "Joseph recognized his brothers, but they did not recognize him. And Joseph remembered the dreams he had dreamed of them. And he said to them, 'You are spies; you have come to see the nakedness of the land'" (Genesis 42:8–9). Joseph could have exacted his revenge on his brothers! Instead, they interacted until finally he revealed his identity to them (Genesis 45:1–3). He could have blamed his brothers for the agony of his life story. Instead, he honored God by forgiving them. It seems that Joseph did not allow himself to be bitter, to wallow in self-pity, or to quit on life. Through this process of being knocked down and getting back up once again, Joseph's character developed as he became a man of God.

> His journey from the bottom of the cistern in his homeland as a young person to now being a man at age 30 and serving Pharaoh had amazing turns, knockdowns, and discouragements. But Joseph kept battling, kept getting back on his feet, and never, ever quit.

- When Joseph finally revealed himself to his brothers, they "could not answer him, for they were dismayed at his presence" (Genesis 45:3). They assumed that they would receive punishment from Joseph, even death. Instead, Joseph responded in kindness to them and honored God. Joseph was no longer the boy they had victimized. He was not a hardened criminal changed by prison life. He rose before them as a man who stood firm in his faith in God. Every time someone knocked him to the canvas of life, he got back to his feet by responding righteously and honoring God.

- Jacob died in Egypt and Joseph's brothers assumed that with their father gone, he would then extract his revenge on them. They lied to Joseph telling him that before he died, their father instructed them to tell Joseph to forgive them. They threw themselves at his feet and declared that they were his slaves (Genesis 50:15–18). But Joseph did not intend to hurt them or make them his slaves. He said to them, "'You meant evil against me, but God meant it for good, to bring it about that many people should be kept alive, as they are today. So do not fear; I will provide for you and your little ones.' Thus he comforted them and spoke kindly to them" (Gen. 50:20–21). Joseph revealed to his brothers that his personal drama was the plan of God. He instructed them to relocate the entire family to Egypt and thus saved them from the famine. The result of Joseph standing firm in the Lord was his personal salvation, and the salvation of his family and the nation of Israel.

There are so many lessons that we can learn from the life of Joseph. Here are some examples of such lessons. I encourage you to add to this list.

1. WHEN LIFE KNOCKS YOU DOWN REMEMBER THE TRUTH THAT GOD IS NOT PUNISHING YOU.

He has not deserted you, and He is not uncaring. We live in a fallen world in which "bad things happen to good people." It is a reality of life. We will not live in a perfect world until we are in heaven. While it is true that God will discipline us because He loves us and that also, we will reap the consequences of our actions, our suffering is not done by a vengeful God. Sometimes, good people are impacted negatively by others acting badly.

2. GOD WILL TAKE THAT WHICH WAS MEANT FOR EVIL AND TURN IT TO ACCOMPLISH HIS WILL.

We must trust this promise and be faithful to Him in our life journey. There will be seasons when it seems that our life story takes a turn for the worse, maybe even multiple times. But even those periods are under God's sight as He is never caught by surprise or unaware of our situation.

3. WHEN OUR LIFE CIRCUMSTANCE IS BLEAK, WE CAN ASK GOD HOW WE ARE TO RESPOND IN A MANNER THAT HONORS HIM.

Then we will grow in our love for Him and in our character. This means that we refuse to be a victim. How easy it would be to become bitter, wallow in self-pity, and quit on life! Instead, we must admit that life has knocked us down and then turn to God. Our questions change from "Why me?" and "Why am I being tested?" to "What can I learn?" and "How can I honor God in this trial?"

4. SEASONS DO NOT LAST FOREVER. "THIS TOO SHALL PASS" IS TRUE.

This is a difficult lesson for many of us to learn. There are times in life, when we have to admit that we are in a difficult circumstance, yet take hope that seasons change for the better if we respond rightly. The fight or flight response comes naturally to us, but our response must be to stand firm and to take life one step at a time. We can win the moment by responding righteously. Then we can win the hour, the day, the week.

5. AT VARIOUS POINTS IN OUR JOURNEY, WE MAY BE TEMPTED TO DEVIATE FROM GOD'S PLAN AND TAKE OUR OWN PATH.

However, this will complicate matters and bring more heartache. We must remain faithful to God regardless of the circumstances.

6. WE CAN STILL FIND LIGHT IN THE MIDST OF LIFE'S STORMS.

Joseph was hated by his brothers, yet he still heard from God in dreams. His brother sold him into slavery, yet he rose to be in charge of Potiphar's household. He was imprisoned wrongly, yet he was put in charge of the prison. So in the middle of your trial, you can still be in the presence of God and discover how you can grow in depth of character in spite of your surroundings.

7. EVEN THOUGH WE MAY NOT SEE THE HAND OF GOD ON US DURING OUR PERSONAL DRAMA, WE MUST REMEMBER THAT GOD IS PRESENT.

He is moving on our behalf, and the best is yet to come.

8. CHOOSE THE RIGHT RESPONSE.

Every time Joseph was knocked down, he chose to get back to his feet and he chose to stand firm. During every turn and downward spiral, he never allowed life to strip him of his faith, his identity in God, or his ability to decide what direction he would pursue. Our chosen responses during our periods of testing can impact us for the rest of our lives. Choose to put on the whole armor of God. Choose to stand firm in truth, righteousness, peace, faith, and hope. Choose to live in the Word of God, pray in the Spirit, and care for others. Choose life!

9. FINALLY, BE DEFINED BY GOD'S VICTORY IN YOUR LIFE AND YOUR CHARACTER THAT HE BUILT IN YOU.

Refuse to be defined by what others have done to you, and instead, be defined by what God has done in you and through you. May your victory anthem be, "Look at what the Lord has done!"

"Therefore, my brother and sisters, you whom I love and long for, my joy and crown, stand firm in the Lord in this way, dear friends!" (Philippians 4:1).